Hermeneutics: A Very Short Introduction

'The Introduction clearly points to the major issues involved in hermeneutics. Jens Zimmermann writes excellently for a wide audience and the references to texting and to digital worlds gives it a contemporary feel.'

Graham Ward, Regius Professor of Divinity,
Christ Church Oxford,
Director of Graduate Studies

'Zimmermann offers one of the best short introductions to modern hermeneutics. The writing is at all times concise, clear and engaging. The author brilliantly evaluates the riches of this major intellectual tradition as well as revealing its ongoing creative influence on contemporary thought.'

Richard Kearney, Charles Seelig Professor at
Boston College and author of Anatheism
and Carnal Hermeneutics

Very Short Introductions available now:

Available soon:

For more information visit our website

www.oup.com/vsi/

Jens Zimmermann

HERMENEUTICS

A Very Short Introduction

OXFORD
UNIVERSITY PRESS

OXFORD
UNIVERSITY PRESS

Great Clarendon Street, Oxford, OX2 6DP,
United Kingdom

Oxford University Press is a department of the University of Oxford.
It furthers the University's objective of excellence in research, scholarship,
and education by publishing worldwide. Oxford is a registered trade mark of
Oxford University Press in the UK and in certain other countries

Published in the United States of America by Oxford University Press
198 Madison Avenue, New York, NY 10016, United States of America

British Library Cataloguing in Publication Data
Data available

Library of Congress Control Number: 2015939572

ISBN 978-0-19-968535-6

Printed and bound by
CPI Group (UK) Ltd, Croydon, CR0 4YY

Contents

Preface

This book is designed to accomplish two things. The first aim is to introduce the non-specialist reader to the idea of hermeneutics as a philosophical school of thought. To familiarize the reader with the discipline of philosophical hermeneutics, I have sketched its historical origins, presented its most important thinkers, and outlined its main claims. The second aim is to show that hermeneutics is a defining trait of our humanity and is foundational to every field of human knowledge. To this end, I have traced the intrinsic role interpretation plays in philosophy, theology, art, law, and science.

Writing a short—indeed *very* short—introduction requires selection, and selection necessitates exclusion. My choice to show how hermeneutics works meant neglecting some theoretical issues and debates in favour of interpretive practices and concrete examples. Thus the reader familiar with hermeneutics will miss some standard critiques of hermeneutics by Emilio Betti, Karl-Otto Apel, Jürgen Habermas, and Paul Ricoeur, or the (mis) appropriation of hermeneutics for pragmatism by Richard Rorty. Instead, I chose to include the broader summary criticism that hermeneutics entails relativism. Those interested in a brief overview of the main philosophical debates about hermeneutics should consult the Appendix, which is written in a more condensed, academic style than the rest of the book. In addition, the Further reading section will direct interested readers to two very good, more conventional introductions to philosophical hermeneutics.

My decision to focus on the practical implications of hermeneutics also influenced topical choices within each knowledge discipline. Thus in theology, for example, I omitted debates between philosophy and theology to focus instead on the connection between theories of inspiration and the nature of the text, which determine interpretive practices. For the same reason, in the law chapter, I have chosen to focus on practical interpretive issues drawn from broader public debates rather than focus on exchanges between legal philosophers. When writing this book, I had in mind both interested general readers who have never heard of hermeneutics, and those of my academic colleagues who are looking for an introductory text that will help their students grasp the essential nature and claims of hermeneutics. Consultation with both general readers and colleagues was essential to the writing of this book.

I dedicate this book to my wife Sabine, whose patient reading, merciless cutting, and constructive criticism greatly improved its quality. I also owe much thanks to Jean Grondin, John Behr, Stephen Dunning, and Robert Doede for commenting on the manuscript. The Very Short Introduction editorial team and external readers were also extremely helpful in shaping this introduction to hermeneutics. All remaining faults are, as always, the author's responsibility.

List of illustrations

Chapter 1
What is hermeneutics?

What is hermeneutics? A simple answer is that it means interpretation. Interpretation occurs in many fields of study and also in day-to-day life. We interpret plays, novels, abstract art, music and movies, employment contracts, the law, the Bible, the Quran, and other sacred texts; but we also interpret the actions of our friends and enemies, or try to figure out what a job termination means in the context of our life story. How and why do we interpret? The goal of interpretation is to make sense of a text or situation, to understand what they mean. This seems to imply that interpretation only becomes necessary when we do not understand something right away. Indeed, the need for interpretation appears more obvious in some cases than in others. For example, most people would agree that plays, novels, legal statutes, and religious texts require interpretation, although some fundamentalists like to affirm the utter clarity of religious texts. We also accept that the Supreme Court interprets the constitution.

Yet in other areas of life, the need for interpretation is less obvious. When you see a red traffic light and stop, is this an interpretation? When a scientist reports on her research, does she just explain what happens in nature or does she interpret nature? Is interpretation—hermeneutics that is—necessary only when misunderstanding requires a special effort on our part to clarify meaning? This assumption seems plausible. After all, 'Hermeneutics' has often stood for a set of interpretive rules designed to clear up difficult textual passages. This book shows, however, that hermeneutics is more than the interpretive principles or methods we resort to when immediate comprehension fails us. Rather, hermeneutics is already unconsciously at work even when we grasp the obvious meaning of a red light. We will see that hermeneutics is the art of understanding and of making oneself understood. In this book, we will concentrate mostly on the art of understanding. One is engaged in hermeneutics whenever one tries to grasp the meaning of something—be it a conversation, a newspaper article, a Shakespeare play, or an account of past events. This book shows that the goal of hermeneutics is understanding, and that although understanding may be guided by analytical principles, it cannot be reduced to them. Understanding requires art rather than rule-governed science. For example, trying to understand why the girl you brought to the party dances with everyone but you involves a unique personal interpretive effort that goes beyond mere logical analysis and general interpretive principles.

We will also see that understanding is something that goes beyond what we nowadays call knowledge: the mere passing or receiving of information. Understanding is knowledge in the deeper sense of grasping not just facts but their integration into a meaningful whole. When you read the word 'breakable' on top of a moving box, why do you handle this box more carefully than other boxes, even though you do not know what is inside? It is because you immediately integrate the word into a meaningful whole that goes beyond mere information, beyond a mere linguistic analysis of the word 'breakable'. You interpret the word based on personal life experience and cultural understanding of property. Thus hermeneutics or interpretation refers to the sort of understanding by which we integrate facts into a meaningful whole, the kind of practical operation that provides knowledge in the sense of deep familiarity with something.

The term *hermeneutics*

The word 'hermeneutics' comes from the ancient Greek language (*hermeneuein* = to utter, to explain, to translate), and was first used by thinkers who discussed how divine messages or mental ideas are expressed in human language. The ancient Greek philosopher Plato (427–347 BCE), for example, used the word *hermeneutics* in dealing with poets as 'hermeneuts of the divine', and his student Aristotle (384–322 BCE) wrote the first extant treatise on hermeneutics, in which he showed how spoken and written words were expressions of inner thoughts. Thus, from its very first appearance, the term *hermeneuein*, along with its later Latin equivalent 'interpretari', was associated with the task of understanding some kind of spoken or written communication.

The word *hermeneutics* has also been associated with the winged-messenger god, Hermes (see Figure 1). In Greek mythology, Hermes relays divine tidings to mortals. While there is little evidence for the still popular etymology that the word *hermeneutics* derives from Hermes, he nevertheless provides a useful emblem for our definition of hermeneutics. Interpretation does involve the deciphering of unclear messages. It is essentially an act of mediation, or translation, and Hermes, who was also described as an eloquent speaker and cunning trickster, represents the need for translation of difficult communications. Hermes reminds us that interpretation involves both grasping what someone has said (receiving a message) and making oneself understood (sending a message). In this book we will focus almost exclusively on the first aspect of receiving communications through texts. The divine figure of Hermes suggests that interpretation is driven by our desire to grasp the existential import of what we are trying to understand. As the philosopher Martin Heidegger (1889–1976), an important figure for modern hermeneutics, put it, 'Hermes is the messenger of the gods. He brings the message of fate.' For Heidegger, hermeneutics was the

1. Hermes, messenger of the gods, as depicted on a Greek vase
c.500–450 BCE. Hermes flies on winged boots, holding his herald's
wand and wearing a traveller's cap and cloak.

kind of interpretation that listened for an important message or announcement of crucial importance. Heidegger's point is that interpretation is motivated by our personal interest and concern. Whether I read the Bible, an employment contract, or try to understand why my friend has not visited me in weeks, I want to know my 'fate', that is, what these texts and actions mean to me. Interpretation, in other words, is intrinsically guided by my present concerns, by the desire to hear an announcement that pertains to my own situation.

Hermeneutics and the quest for self-understanding

From its inception in Greek antiquity, hermeneutics aimed to discover the truth about ourselves and the world we inhabit for the sake of wisdom. Especially in ancient times, philosophers argued that discoveries about the nature of things should enhance our understanding of who we are and how we should live our lives as human beings. They thought that all understanding is ultimately self-understanding. In his philosophical dialogues, for example, Plato taught that human knowledge is principally about self-understanding and moral formation. In Plato's dialogues, the figure of Socrates epitomizes this philosophical attitude. In Socrates' *Apology*, his self-defence during his trial for allegedly corrupting Athens' youth, Socrates proclaimed life's highest goal to be a soul perfected by wisdom and virtue through rational self-examination. 'An unexamined life,' he asserted, 'is not a human life.'

In contrast to our modern inclination to discount philosophy, religion, and poetry as sources of real knowledge, the ancient world considered them to be important carriers of moral ideals. Homer's poetry, for instance, was thought to teach courage and striving for excellence but also to warn against pride. Aristotle famously argued that poetry was more elevated than history because poems went beyond mere facts to imagine the purpose of human development and deduce universal moral truths. Poetry shared this distinction with rhetoric, the art of persuasion, on the basis of cogent reasoning. Both Aristotle and Plato recognized the potential danger of rhetoric to degenerate into emotional pleading or verbal pyrotechnics to win an argument at the expense of truth. Even in the ancient world, it seems, there were lawyers who thrived on this malpractice. Generally, however, the ancients believed that rhetoric's true purpose was the attainment and teaching of deep truths about the human condition. One of the questions we will try to answer in this introduction to hermeneutics is why art, poetry, and rhetoric were regarded as important sources of knowledge in determining the human condition well into the 17th century, while many modern thinkers tend to exclude them.

Hermeneutics as philosophical discipline

So far we have defined hermeneutics as a basic human activity of interpretation concerned with understanding the meaning of communications or life situations. The word 'hermeneutics', however, has a second meaning. It is also the name for the philosophical discipline concerned with analysing the conditions for understanding. Hermeneutic philosophers examine, for example, how our cultural traditions, our language, and our nature as historical beings make understanding possible. Philosophical hermeneutics has many antecedents but emerged as its own discipline in the 20th century with the publication of the German philosopher Hans-Georg Gadamer's book, *Truth and Method* (1960), which was subtitled 'fundamental contours of a hermeneutic philosophy'. Gadamer developed his hermeneutic philosophy by interacting with a number of major figures in the history of hermeneutics we will also discuss in this book: Friedrich Daniel Schleiermacher, Wilhelm Dilthey, Martin Heidegger, Rudolf Bultmann, and Paul Ricoeur.

It is important to make clear from the outset that philosophical hermeneutics is not a particular *theory* of knowledge. A theory seeks to isolate methods of interpretation in order to come up with regulative principles that allow us to control the production of meaning. For example, a theory of legal interpretation will try to establish rules for the interpretation of legal texts. Similarly, a literary theory of interpretation, such as feminist theory or Marxist theory, will prescribe principles for regulating our reading of literary texts. In this sense, theories have a practical goal. No doubt, every field of knowledge, whether in the human or natural sciences, represents a certain mode of knowing, and thus follows a particular methodology that corresponds to its particular object of study. The philosophical discipline of hermeneutics, however, is not a method aiming at a specific practical goal or particular reading. Rather, hermeneutic philosophers are interested in understanding as such: how and under what conditions does understanding happen? Philosophical hermeneutics, as Gadamer himself put it, is concerned with 'understanding understanding'. As a philosophical discipline, hermeneutics examines and describes what happens when understanding of any kind takes place.

What is understanding?

Hermeneutic thinkers argue that understanding is the interpretive act of integrating particular things such as words, signs, and events into a meaningful whole. We understand an object, word, or fact when it makes sense within our own life context and thus speaks to us meaningfully. When we understand objects, texts, or situations in this way, they become part of our inner mental world so that we can express them again in our own terms. We have not understood a poem, for example, when we can merely repeat the words by heart; rather we demonstrate understanding when we intone the words meaningfully and are able to express the poem's ideas in our own words.

Hermeneutic thinkers believe that in most cases understanding as this kind of integration happens unconsciously, because we already move in a familiar cultural environment within which we perceive words and objects in a pre-established context of meaning. Our modern culture tends to think that real knowledge consists in quantification, that is, in the scientific numerical description of things in the world. On this account, objective truth requires an impersonal, theoretical stance toward things. Hermeneutic philosophers contend, on the contrary, that our primary mode of perception is not theoretical but practical, and depends on our current desires or interests.

Imagine for a moment that you want to attend a concert or play. After parking the car and walking six city blocks on a cold, rainy evening, and while lining up at the entrance for another half hour, you glimpse an inviting auditorium seat. The seat appears to you not as a meaningless object of neutral observation but as a place of comfort where you can rest and warm your weary bones while enjoying the anticipated performance. You do not first perceive this seat from a purely objective stance in terms of its compositional material or its measurements. Such a theoretical stance is not our primary mode of perception, but a secondary, unnatural way of looking at things we adopt when we abstract something from the context of our experience to study it separately. Should, for example, the seat collapse under us as we sat down, only then would we adopt a scientific attitude and examine the seat to determine its structure and the reasons for its malfunction.

If hermeneutic philosophers are right in believing that this practical understanding is our primary mode of perception, then the way we perceive the world as meaningful is closer to our experience of art than to a science experiment. When we enjoy a performance of Shakespeare's *Hamlet*, for example, or study the text of this play, we intuitively grasp that we encounter not contemporary reality but a play that arises from the social and political milieu of old England. If we were professional critics, we could also analyse the archaic language of the play, long-lost allusions, and wordplays that would deepen our grasp of the play's inner dynamic. Yet beyond any of these details, we enjoy the play and may be led into a deeper study of it because Shakespeare speaks to us. We are drawn into the play because it tells us something about our present human condition, with emotions and situations that are already familiar to us. *Hamlet* speaks to us of betrayal, opportunism, and false loves. *Othello* confronts us with the tragedy of misplaced trust and the power of jealousy. As we will see in the coming chapters, hermeneutic thinkers argue that our ability to understand a play from roughly 400 years ago has to do with the way our human condition, history, tradition, and especially language enable us to receive such a play or a text from the past.

Interpreting animals

While we have used the word 'activity' to describe understanding as the interpretive act of integrating things into a meaningful whole, hermeneutic philosophers argue that interpretation is not only something we do but also something we *are*. Interpretation is not an occasional luxury but our fundamental way of being in the world. We are 'interpreting animals', and human knowing always entails interpretation, whether we are dealing with a Shakespearean play or a hypothesis in physics. Now, someone might object that knowledge consists in ascertaining facts, while interpretation is not about knowing real facts but about determining meaning. As we shall see in the chapter on science, this neat distinction between knowledge of facts and understanding of meaning is highly problematic. Imagine an alien scientist, who finds a broken toaster and tries to fix it. Even if the alien analyses all the nuts and bolts of the toaster, knowledge of these details alone will not help him understand their function within the combined whole of a bread toasting machine designed to enhance a human breakfast. He might possibly fix the toaster, but not understand its purpose. For all he knows, this might be a machine for ejecting pre-warmed, small plates before dinner.

Philosophical hermeneutics, in other words, stands for a certain conviction about the nature and communication of truth, namely that all understanding is a matter of interpretation and that

**"Honey, when you say we can't communicate...
what exactly do you mean?"**

2. Communication and interpretation.

interpretation is essentially the personal integration of objects or words into a meaningful whole. True knowledge that involves understanding is not ultimately rule governed because our whole life experience conditions our insights in a way that is irreducible to method. I can memorize a map or a set of rules about map reading and still get lost because I cannot integrate the information with the terrain itself or personally grasp the conventions of map reading. Meaningful knowledge and communication require more than mere information exchange and cannot be mastered by mere technique. They require the personal integration of details into a meaningful whole—they require interpretation. As the cartoon indicates (see Figure 2), sometimes even the clearest statements hold deep existential meanings that cannot be explained by rules of logic or language.

The three central claims of hermeneutics

Hermeneutics as a philosophical field of study is a wide disciplinary tent that accommodates a great variety of philosophers, theologians, and literary and legal theorists from the past and the present who have written about interpretation. We can grasp their shared interests when we define *hermeneutic thinkers* as those who are concerned more specifically with the universal conditions for human understanding in three areas: the nature of consciousness, the nature of truth, and the importance of language. Hermeneutic philosophers believe that in each of these vital areas of our experience, key developments in modern thought and culture have brought about a distorted view of who we are and how we arrive at knowledge.

Consciousness: the self is no island

Hermeneutic thinkers claim that our modern consciousness has been shaped in such a way that we imagine ourselves as islands of awareness floating in the grand ocean of life, disconnected from other selves. We tend to think of the mind as something interior, separated from the outside material world. From this inner island, or bubble, we reach out to make contact with others and with the world around us. In philosophical terms, we are individual subjects confronted by external objects, such as nature or other people. We don't often reflect on the problems of such a view because it rather agrees with our sense of self-sufficiency and individual freedom. We like to think that no one tells us what to do, and that we make up our own minds after considering all the evidence in a completely unbiased way. On this view, ideas, concepts, and even historical events appear as if passing on a conveyor belt before our mind's eye, from which we take what we consciously decide to make our own.

The Canadian philosopher and hermeneutic thinker Charles Taylor helpfully labelled this specious self-contained consciousness a 'disengaged self', because outside influences are admitted only by conscious choice. Hermeneutic thinkers, by contrast, believe in an 'engaged self' that is fundamentally connected to the world and to other people. They argue that consciousness itself is shaped by the way in which we inhabit the world. The universal human experiences of birth, death, hunger, and the need for shelter already determine how we see the world and undergird the formation of every particular culture. Moreover, culture, language, and upbringing shape our attitudes long before we make conscious decisions. The community or tradition to which we belong gives us the lenses through which we see the world.

Truth is an event

Our view of consciousness naturally informs our understanding of truth and how we obtain it. Based on the assumption of separation between mind and world, the disengaged self naturally favours disengaged reason. Disengaged reason is the kind of abstract, theoretical view of truth we know from a scientific laboratory: a detached observer arrives at an insight by setting up a methodical experiment, and will arrive at the same result every time the same methodical procedure is repeated. Here knowledge is the result of method and empirically verifiable repetition. Objective knowledge is defined as the result of this disinterested observation. Hermeneutic thinkers, however, believe that we have falsely elevated this scientific ideal of knowledge, allowing it to become the measure of all human knowledge. They contest the idea that knowledge is obtained through disinterested observation. Rather, hermeneutic thinkers say that we only conduct experiments and want to know about the world because we are already deeply involved in it at the level of everyday, practical activity. Without this prior experiential relation to things, scientific results would be meaningless. As the Scottish philosopher John Macmurray (1891–1976) pointed out, 'If we did not know what water is by drinking it and boiling it in our kettles, the scientific statement that water is H_2O would be merely a meaningless noise.'

For hermeneutics, knowledge is more than naming and describing objects; it involves understanding meaningful structures we already participate in. This is not only true in the case of science, but also in the humanities and social sciences. Let's take, for example, the study of history. Disengaged-self people argue that we dispassionately observe history from the outside and present merely the facts to arrive at objective truth about past events. By contrast, hermeneutic thinkers argue that the reason we can understand history in the first place is because we are historical beings through and through. We are part of history and shaped by it. Disengaged-self people argue that we should suppress our personal beliefs or prejudices in order to escape the ideological blinders of tradition. Those who champion a hermeneutic view of truth, however, object that past texts or events hold meaning for us in the first place because we stand within a tradition that has provided us with the very concepts through which we are connected to the past in a meaningful way.

When, for example, we read Plato's dialogues on law and government, we do so as people whose lives have been profoundly shaped by other readers of these texts. We enter into a long-standing conversation on just laws and governance, a conversation in which Plato's reflections have shaped constitutions all over the world, including that of the United States. This is simply to say that we see the world through the eyes our cultural traditions provide for us. Without these conceptual lenses that allow us meaningful access to reality, we would be blind. Hermeneutic thinkers hold that we arrive at truth because we already participate in something greater that conveys truth to us, such as the language and cultural tradition we inhabit. It is therefore misleading to pretend such influence does not exist or to repress it for the sake of supposed objectivity. Such repression blinds us to our guiding influences and thus prevents us from understanding why we believe what we believe. Thus, ironically, obsession with objectivity can entrap us in subjectivism. Instead, hermeneutic thinkers insist that we need to redefine objective truth as something we take part in rather than something we merely observe from a distance. We don't make truth happen; rather truth is something that happens to us. Truth is an event.

The importance of language

For disengaged-self people and their theoretical, detached way of seeing the world, language is like a toolbox of labels we attach to things in order to handle them. Words and the ideas expressed through them are instruments that help us communicate our needs, obtain things, persuade others to give us what we want, and allow us to describe and control our world. This instrumental conception of language flows naturally from the division between our perception of the world (as so many objects external to us) and the images or linguistic expressions we use to designate these objects. Perception and language are kept apart. The common expression to speak nothing but the 'naked truth' fittingly illustrates this separation of truth from the uncertainties of language. This demand for 'naked truth' stems from Thomas Sprat (1635–1713), an English clergyman and member of the royal scientific society, who was so enamoured with the clarity of scientific language that he wanted to strip truth of any images or metaphors to grant us access to how things really are. That Sprat himself had to use the image of nakedness to make his point is a pretty good indication that language and its images are more central to perception than he was willing to admit.

A common objection to the universal claim of hermeneutics that all understanding is a matter of interpretation is that our immediate sense experience of the world precedes any interpretation. For example, we have a toothache, or we sense heat, before we can put these sensations into words and interpret them. Hermeneutic thinkers don't deny this immediate experience; they do deny, however, that we can have a *meaningful* experience without understanding pain or temperature first within a cultural vocabulary by which we make sense of things. Just think of the way in which languages express the same sense experience differently: In English, I *am* cold. In French, I *have* cold (*j'ai froid*), and in

German, it *is* cold *to me* (*mir ist kalt*). While relating the same sense experience of coldness, each linguistic variation expresses a different relation of the self to the world.

The language we use already interprets for us a certain way in which we relate to sense experience and how we express it to others. For this reason, hermeneutic thinkers argue that language guides our perception intrinsically. For them, language includes any images, signs, or symbols by which we understand and communicate our experience of the world. They believe that our perception of the world and our thought depends on an intricate linguistic web of words and concepts that develop historically over time. Words and terms we inherit through our upbringing provide guiding concepts for our recognition of meaningful human experience.

This symbolic universe into which we are inducted from childhood on provides what hermeneutic philosophers call our *pre-understanding* of the things we interpret. Moreover, according to hermeneutics, language gives us humans the unique ability to abstract images from immediate sense experience to develop sophisticated concepts and ideas, such as justice, freedom, equality, legal systems, and the like. Because of this linguistic ability, we are able to preserve and pass on our cultural achievements to subsequent generations. In early oral cultures, this transmission took place through stories. Especially through the later inventions of writing, texts, and libraries, we are able to store and communicate our cultural achievements. Language lies at the root of this astounding ability to transmit culture. Hermeneutic thinkers claim that naked truth does not exist. Rather, our experience of the world and our reflections about the world always occur through images, concepts, and words. In short, the world is given to us already interpreted through language. Language, as Martin Heidegger famously put it, is 'the house of being'.

Is 'hermeneutics' another word for relativism?

Hermeneutics makes the universal claim that we are interpreting animals. Interpretation is not an optional activity, something we do every now and then when the naked facts aren't clear. The only way we can ever experience the world as meaningful is through interpretation. To perceive is to interpret. Many misunderstand this universal claim that all knowledge is interpretive to signal the denial of objective truth and to invite the spectre of relativism. Relativism is the concept that whatever we hold to be true has no absolute, universal validity but is relative to our personal historical and cultural circumstances. The fear of relativism crops up whenever people talk about interpretation, especially in debates about ethics. Moral relativism means that all moral claims are simply cultural conventions that can be changed at any time. According to this view, your mother's rule to keep your elbows off the table at dinner would carry the same moral weight as the United Nation's Universal Declaration of Human Rights.

When people learn that I teach hermeneutics and believe in a hermeneutic view of truth, a common response is, 'So you're a relativist, right?' The argument underlying this response is usually something like this: hermeneutics basically means interpretation, and interpretation is what we do until we really figure something out and arrive at objective, final, indisputable knowledge. The claim is that we interpret subjectively and produce merely personal opinion, but we know objectively and arrive at true, impartial knowledge. Surely, we have all heard the comment, 'Ah but that's not how it really is. That's just your interpretation of the matter.' This sentiment conveys an image of truth as something that rests on fixed rules and formulas, not unlike mathematics. After all, two plus two is four, no matter who looks at the equation, and we can fly airplanes because our technology relies on empirically proven, unchanging physical laws that are the same for everyone. Given this model of truth, interpretation is opposed to *real* knowledge. So when someone claims that knowledge is *always* a matter of interpretation, this person must be a relativist who believes that objective truth is impossible and that all we have are competing, mutually exclusive truth claims. Ultimately, binding truth would then be decided by convention or by force.

Hermeneutics rejects this simple opposition of impartial objective truth on the one hand, and subjective opinion on the other. Fortunately, even many scientists today question this opposition, which stems itself from the now widely discredited view that scientific discoveries rest purely on experimental method and strictly rule-governed, impersonal observation by which we carefully pile knowledge upon knowledge until a discovery is obtained. For a long time, this scientific method was accepted as the gold standard of truth for which every knowledge discipline should strive. Today, however, many academics and scientists have come to believe that this gold standard has proven to be a golden calf, the false idol of 'scientific objectivism', which we worshipped for a while, but which is now exposed and deposed for its distortion of how knowledge works.

While the scientific method continues to remain an important tool, scientists have realized that the process of discovery is much more intuitive and uncontrolled than formerly imagined. Now, objectivism and relativism appear as two sides of the same coin. Both extremes are based on the same faulty concept of objectivity. So with this toppling of the simple opposition between subjective and objective truth, a position beyond objectivism and relativism became possible. At least among many scholars there is now an emerging consensus to regard the attainment of objective truth less like watching a spectator sport and more like playing a game. In a board game or a tennis match, there are rules and conventions one must observe to play, but at the same time, each performance is unique and requires passionate involvement to succeed. It is only by being deeply involved that any understanding of the play can take place. For hermeneutic thinkers, this is how all knowledge works. Objective understanding of the world, others, and ourselves requires personal engagement and passionate curiosity.

Acknowledging personal engagement in obtaining knowledge does not invite relativism. After all, to claim that all knowledge is relative to a personal standpoint, is not at all the same as claiming that only individual perspectives exist and are all of equal value. It is only to claim that we are not gods who look down on our world, but finite creatures deeply affected by the course of history. The hermeneutic claim that our knowledge is always relative to a certain context and personal viewpoint would only be relativism if we actually were isolated selves, unformed by history or language. In truth, however, our standpoint always includes a universally valid context of meaning, or what philosophers call a 'horizon'. Of course, what exactly this shared horizon consists of is a much-debated question. For most hermeneutic thinkers, this horizon is the tradition and language we inhabit, and through which we share a meaningful world. While they admit that our ways of seeing the world are culturally dependent, they also acknowledge universally shared human conditions that give rise to transcultural experiences, such as evil, sacrifice or love, that allow for the translation of our particular cultural symbols. Most hermeneutic thinkers are firm believers in universal reason that allows for translation between all languages and cultures. To understand is to interpret: this universal claim of hermeneutics is not relativism but the admission that we are not gods.

Chapter 2
Hermeneutics: a brief history

The history of hermeneutics is a conversation about knowledge.
As soon as we pronounce the word 'interpretation', we are entering
into a long-standing conversation about what constitutes valid
knowledge. Simply by asking the question 'what is hermeneutics?'
we are joining a discussion about the nature of human knowledge,
a conversation that connects ancient and modern conceptions
of knowledge.

Knowledge in the ancient world

In the ancient world, knowledge was much more unified than
it is today. Not only mathematics and logic, but also poetry,
rhetoric, and philosophy were counted as important sources of
objective truth. In fact, for the ancient Greek and Roman
civilizations, the transmission of knowledge depended largely
on the preservation and interpretation of authoritative texts.
Philosophical, religious, and literary texts, such as those written
by Homer or Virgil, had quasi-sacred status because they were
regarded as having captured essential insights into human nature.
These texts were carefully preserved and commented on from one
generation to the next, a practice that eventually led to the
invention of libraries and helped establish basic interpretive
principles that are still valid today. Education in the ancient world
consisted of the students' immersion in such texts and their

commentaries for the purpose of self-knowledge. The ultimate goal of interpreting texts was character formation.

It is important for us moderns to understand the reason for the ancients' love of words and texts as carriers of wisdom. For Plato, and indeed for most ancient thinkers, human language was capable of revealing universal truths about ourselves and the world because human reason participated in an intelligible universe. Philosophers figured that the cosmos was shaped by divine powers and thus inherently rational. Embedded in a rationally structured cosmos, the mind could tap into a logical structure and moral order that provided universally valid insights for self-understanding. People back then thought that the best of human wisdom or human law reflected this cosmic order. The Roman statesman and philosopher Marcus Aurelius (CE 121–80) summed up this belief when he wrote, 'for there is one universe out of all, one God through all, one substance and one law, one common reason of all intelligent creatures and one truth'.

The ancient Greek word for this 'common reason' was *Logos*, which later Latin writers translated variously as *verbum* (word or speech) or *ratio* (reason). These terms are all interrelated because they assume a very basic but very crucial point for interpretation, namely that we need language to think and that our reasoning reflects a reality in which things are meaningfully interconnected. In the ancient world, the universe speaks, in a sense, and human words participate in its universal grammar and are therefore a reliable vehicle for the discovery of universal truths. Philosophy, religion, poetry, the arts, and literature are important because human words (*logoi*) shared in cosmic reason (*logos*).

Jewish theologians equated the cosmic '*Logos*' with the creative power of God, and thus opened up the way for Christianity's interpretation of Christ as the eternal power and wisdom of God, who, Christians believed, had become a human being. This theological move guaranteed that human language could share in divine truth, and ensured that Europe remained essentially an interpretive, word-centred culture that revolved around the creation, compilation, and interpretation of authoritative religious, literary, and legal texts well into the 17th century. Our sketch of knowledge in the ancient world shows us the intrinsic connection between mind and world assumed by pre-modern interpreters. This connection grounded the authority of texts, explained the importance of tradition, and accounted for the capacity of words to mirror, however imperfectly, the cosmic order shared by the human spirit.

From wisdom to epistemology

The breakdown of the link between the human mind and the world, which occurred by degrees from the 14th century onward, fundamentally altered the ancient view of knowledge. Many social and political factors contributed to this breakdown. Some of the most important were what we may call conflicts of interpretation. Take science and religion, for example. For centuries, science and religion had been harmonized through the interpretive framework of 'two books'. The belief that God had authored both the book of nature and the Bible meant that science could never be the enemy of religion. Yet when Copernicus suggested that the earth orbits the sun, he broke with the Aristotelian geocentric interpretation of the universe posited as biblical by the medieval Christian church.

Moreover, animosity and even wars among the dominant Christian confessions themselves also raised the question: whose interpretation of truth was the right one? How could one obtain a firm foundation for true knowledge? This anxiety about certain truth gave rise to *foundationalism*, that is, the attempt to find an unshakeable foundation for knowledge: an indubitable, certain bedrock of truth on which one could then pile, Lego-style, knowledge upon knowledge. With this anxiety about certainty, the conversation about knowledge changed from a concern for

wisdom to a preoccupation with *epistemeology* that is, with
theories about correct knowledge. The ancients asked how
knowledge could enable a virtuous life. Moderns focus more on
the epistemological question how we can know that something is
true. The emphasis shifts from edification to verification.

Separating the mind from the world

The French mathematician and philosopher René Descartes
(1596–1650) illustrates this modern attitude towards knowledge. In
order to obtain certain knowledge, Descartes doubted everything
the ancient world had considered reliable sources of knowledge:
truths handed down by tradition, religious or worldly authorities,
the body, emotions, and the senses. As Descartes put it, true
knowledge belongs to those 'who have the ability and the desire
to withdraw from the senses and at the same time from all
prejudices'. What remains is a mind hived off from the world,
aware of the only thing of which it is certain: the act of thinking
itself. From this certainty as the single reliable starting point,
Descartes entrusted to human reason the construction of a sure
edifice of knowledge, from one certain idea to the next. This is
rationalism: the reasoning mind constructs a castle of verities,
brick by conceptual brick, disconnected from life and other minds.

There is something deeply admirable in Descartes's call to
independent, critical thinking, and in his optimism that reason
alone can determine truth. Roughly one hundred years after
Descartes, the German philosopher Immanuel Kant (1724–1804)
articulated a similar sentiment for his cultural period called
'The Enlightenment'. For Kant, intellectual maturity meant the
independence of reason from tradition. At the same time,
however, Descartes's foundationalism bequeathed a serious
problem to philosophy. Descartes purchased the certainty of
rational truths at the price of splitting the mind from the world,
leaving us with the problem of verification: how do I know
whether my inner beliefs are indeed true to reality 'out there'?

This breach between the mind and the world has two important implications for hermeneutics. The first is a redefinition of objective knowledge as unbiased, value-free fact. When it was first used in medieval theories about knowledge, the Latin word *objectivus* simply indicated the appearance of an object to the mind. Only after Descartes do we assume that knowing objectively means to screen out the context of our own lives in order to attain certain knowledge. Eventually, people came to think that the only way to fulfil this requirement for true knowledge was through the scientific method of the empirical sciences. Most of our current divisions between knowledge and belief, reason and faith, science and religion stem from this historical development.

The second important implication of the breach between mind and world is the problem of how to access other minds. The entire text-based, interpretive culture we have inherited from antiquity assumes that literary, historical, legal, and theological texts contain expressions of other minds, either divine or human. Past and present authors' insights about reality could be grasped by later readers because all minds were linked beyond time or culture by participating in a meaningful universe. With the separation of mind and world, however, the interpreter is now faced by a gulf between his own and the author's mind. Modern interpreters experience a double anxiety. How can I validate my perception of the world? And how can I validate my perception of what another has said? Even if Descartes's foundationalism worked logically, his certainty exists only in the world of thought, and a gulf separates the certainties of the inner mind from the outer world of history and other minds. How can this gulf be bridged? Modern hermeneutics is essentially a series of attempts to answer this question.

The beginning of general hermeneutics

The German theologian Daniel Friedrich Schleiermacher (1768–1834) was one of the first modern thinkers who attempted to heal the breach between mind and world. Schleiermacher reasserted the unity of all human knowledge in order to resolve the growing conflict between science and religion. This conflict began to split society into educated people who, adhering to a scientific view of knowledge, deemed religion irrational, and traditional religionists, who struggled to find scientific proofs for their beliefs. Schleiermacher realized that this conflict stemmed from a deficient view of human knowledge. With uncanny prescience, he warned that failing to address this modern obsession with certainty would create a society dominated by culture wars between secular and religious fundamentalists, each believing itself to have the monopoly on truth. A prophetic warning indeed!

Schleiermacher's strategy for avoiding a possible clash between religion and science was to focus on the universal human conditions for understanding that formed the ground of all knowledge disciplines. One needed a general hermeneutic, a theory of understanding as the common basis for the existing rules of interpretation specific to theology, law, and historical studies. Schleiermacher suggested that these particular approaches are merely individual instances of human dialogue in general. The question that unites all these separate interpretive theories is *how do I understand anything spoken or written by someone else?* I hear a string of words, but when I pay attention, I suddenly grasp not only the meaning of each word but also what the speaker means to convey to me. What is the mysterious process by which a hearer suddenly understands what someone else is saying? How is it that I seem to be able to connect to the mind of another human being and do so even across the barriers of time and language?

Hermeneutics of the spirit

Schleiermacher was part of an intellectual movement in Germany called Romanticism. Romantics opposed the dry, rationalist view of reality inherited from Descartes and appealed to what they called *Spirit* (*Geist* in German), a word that could also mean 'mind'. Spirit or *world-Spirit* (*Weltgeist*) meant a kind of creative, intelligent life force that sustained the cosmos, animating both human beings and nature. Not entirely unlike the ancient concept of *Logos* discussed earlier, Spirit was often defined as the pervasive rational-moral power through which all things were interconnected. The German poet Goethe, for example, in depicting an encounter between the restless knowledge seeker Faust with the spirit-world, described this Spirit as the power that is pulsing through every dimension of life, 'weaving God's living garment'. In establishing his general hermeneutic, Schleiermacher appealed to this power as the interconnecting ground of all human understanding, even across time and language.

Schleiermacher and the hermeneutic circle

Long before Schleiermacher, interpreters had established the maxim that understanding any statement depends on a circular movement between part and whole. A text, for example, consists of sentences that make up the text as a whole, and the whole text defines the meaning of each part. A word only has meaning within a sentence, a sentence only within a passage, a passage only within a chapter, a chapter only within a book, a book only within an author's work as a whole, and an author's work as a whole within a certain historical or life context.

Every careful reader knows that the meaning of a particular statement depends on the larger context: a whole within which the part has meaning. It may be less obvious that we usually intuit such a larger context based on trained expectations. Let's say, for example, you pick up Shakespeare's *Hamlet* for the first time. Looking at the book, you probably know that it's a play of the kind we call tragedy and contains the line 'to be or not to be: that is the question'. You have heard this line many times before, in sitcoms or even advertisements. All these prior influences shape your expectations of this play in some way. The hermeneutic circle means that *some* greater context always influences how we understand a particular part. As you read, however, you will have to revise not only your view of what the play is about but also what this famous line actually means. The point is that whole and part influence each other. Our better understanding of particular lines will reshape our grasp of the whole.

Schleiermacher's unique contribution to the hermeneutic conversation about knowledge is his expansion of this textual principle to every aspect of human understanding. He believed that human reasoning, no matter in what area of life, always operates according to this circular movement between part and whole. Schleiermacher thus took a first important step towards an *ontology* of understanding. Ontology is the study of reality or being. Schleiermacher was one of the first thinkers who examined systematically how understanding depends ultimately on the nature of reality and the kind of being we are, rather than on a set of rules. For him, the greater whole that guarantees the unity of knowledge is a universe in which all things are interconnected through Spirit. Being and thought, or world and Spirit, were interdependent for Schleiermacher, both in the macrocosm of the world and the microcosm of human communication. He called the world 'the artwork of the Spirit, the mirror it created of itself', and said that the human spirit participates in this unity that drives all our curiosity, no matter what particular area of reality we happen to study.

According to Schleiermacher, we have a deep sense that all our knowing depends on some unspecifiable great unifying ground of reality. He called this sense our 'feeling of absolute dependence', or, more religiously, our 'god-consciousness'. The notion of god-consciousness was Schleiermacher's answer to the modern fragmentation of knowledge. He argued that even those who do not actually believe in gods nonetheless assume that what they know reflects part of a greater meaningful whole. He believed that by completing our understanding of the universe, every science deals with a particular facet of the Spirit's unified artwork, and thus contributes to our knowledge of God. Ultimately, not only science and art, but also science and religion, are grounded in the same unifying whole and therefore not inherently at loggerheads.

In Schleiermacher's hermeneutic circle of understanding, every great artistic, scientific, or religious insight provides a partial glimpse into the shared cosmic whole. In other words, we can attain knowledge of the universe or of God only through the particular thoughts of others, through concepts, through comparative religions and worldviews. This holistic view of reality would mean, for example, that unified field theory in physics, Jesus's command to love one's enemy, and Shakespeare's warning against the destructive power of jealousy in *Othello* all contribute to our knowledge of reality. For Schleiermacher, any such expressions of the human spirit could in turn be grasped only through the particulars of language and a person's entire life context. This emphasis on the particular explains why Schleiermacher's rather mystical sounding concept of 'Spirit' as the unifying ground for human understanding produced a sober and sophisticated approach to textual interpretation.

Interpretation as reconstruction

Schleiermacher regarded literary or religious texts as the linguistic expression of a mind touched by the world-Spirit. Thus the interpreter's task was to move back through the words to the thoughts of the author, to reconstruct the author's state of mind at the point of writing in order to determine what overall intention determined every other part of the text. Interpretation thus demanded first of all great linguistic sensitivity. Schleiermacher was convinced that thinking and language were intrinsically connected. Thought happened only *as* language, and therefore the interpreter's reconstructive effort required first of all grammatical skills. In translating a New Testament passage, for example, the interpreter had to know ancient Greek well enough to catch every nuance, and possess familiarity with the author's historical context to avoid reading modern meanings into an ancient text.

Yet Schleiermacher also knew that the logic of grammar alone does not account for understanding. Somehow the reader makes an intuitive leap into the meaningful relation of part and whole. This is what Schleiermacher called the 'divinatory' dimension of interpretation. This divinatory act requires, beyond linguistic analysis, personal identification with the thing the author talks about. For this reason, Schleiermacher also called the 'divinatory' reconstruction of another's mental experience the 'psychological' aspect of interpretation, because the reader empathizes with the author's state of mind.

Schleiermacher—pros and cons

Schleiermacher's attempt to heal the breach between mind and world moves the conversation about knowledge back from epistemology to ontology. Rather than focusing on how a statement conveys truth (epistemology), he enquired more generally into who we are as beings who understand (ontology), and what the conditions for understanding are. By making personal conversation the basic model for his general hermeneutics, Schleiermacher drew attention to the relational aspects of interpretation. Interpretation is always about someone communicating something to someone else. A message is passed from person to person, whose life contexts and intentions shape the meaning of a statement. Thus, linguistic rules or interpretive methods alone are not enough to understand another's message.

Moreover, language is far more than a mere instrument of expression. Schleiermacher already knew that neither the speaker nor the interpreter merely reaches for words the way we reach for a tool in our toolbox, but that words are the flesh and blood by which our notions about anything gain form and life. We think in language. Later hermeneutic thinkers have honoured Schleiermacher for these insights but also criticized his reconstructive ideal, namely that interpretation requires stepping out of one's own mind into that of the author. Schleiermacher, these critics say, did well to highlight the author's historical context, but what about our own? Did he not suggest a kind of 'out of body experience' or soul travel for the interpreter, implying that the interpreter can leave her own context behind when entering another's mental world? How can we assert the connection between minds without ignoring the problem of history? This question becomes the central concern of our next hermeneutic thinker.

Dilthey's hermeneutics of life experience

Like Schleiermacher, the literary historian and philosopher Wilhelm Dilthey (1833–1911) sought to overcome the separation of mind and world that characterizes the modern ideal of knowledge. Unlike Schleiermacher, however, Dilthey rejected any appeal to realities beyond this world, such as to a cosmic world-Spirit or any other metaphysical ground for the unity of human knowledge. Rather than appealing to metaphysics—that is to some unchanging essential principles that lie behind human experiences in this world—he argued instead that the firm ground for human knowledge is life experience itself. Not Schleiermacher's cosmic Spirit, but the human spirit that shapes culture becomes the foundation of hermeneutics.

By suggesting that life itself is the bedrock of meaning, Dilthey criticized the two rival contenders for certain knowledge already encountered, namely rationalism and empirical science. On the one hand, Descartes had argued that certain knowledge exists only in rational principles of the mind. Yet, his rationalism cannot do justice to our experience of reality because we do not encounter the world as abstract theoretical deductions, nor do human relations correspond to the numeric certainty of mathematics. On the other hand, empirical scientists claimed that we obtain factual knowledge only through an experimental method with verifiable results. Human freedom, will, and emotions, however, do not conform to the laws of physics.

Dilthey concluded that both rationalists and empiricists pursue an unnatural way of knowing. They assume some value-neutral, impersonal world on which we impose meaning. Dilthey denied that we experience the world as naked facts that have in themselves no value or meaning. He held, on the contrary, that the world is given to us only *as already meaningful* experience. From childhood, we move about understandingly in a common world of human life experience on which the human spirit has left its creative imprint. Whether in the cultivation of nature expressed by our homes, cities, and fields, or the moral values exhibited by family and legal orders, the reality we try to understand exists only as the world of life experience as shaped by the human spirit. Thus, if we want to obtain correct knowledge about the world as we truly experience it, we need a human science that interprets life experience.

Explanation and understanding

Dilthey's life ambition was to give knowledge in the humanities the same kind of respectability enjoyed by the natural sciences. He thought to achieve this goal by a division of labour. The Natural sciences *explain* nature, but only the human sciences can *understand* culture. He argued that the sciences approach the world the way we approach a complex machine, trying to explain its parts and how they work. The empirical sciences' preoccupation with natural forces and laws may be adequate to explain the workings of nature, but the natural sciences are incapable of capturing how the inner world of human spirit, that is how wills, emotions, and ambitions shape the material world to produce culture. We perceive the human world of culture not primarily in terms of mechanisms but in relational terms.

For example, Science can explain what a castle consists of, but it cannot explain why humans would want or need to build a castle in the first place. We are able to penetrate this human world only through *understanding* the expression of life, that is, through deciphering (i.e. interpreting) the imprint of the human spirit on the material world. This work of understanding is the interpretive task of what Dilthey called 'the sciences of the mind' (*Geisteswissenschaften*) or the *human* sciences.

Interpreting à la Dilthey

Dilthey believed that knowledge in the human sciences was objective because, in contrast to Schleiermacher's hermeneutic, the interpreter no longer sought to enter another person's mind, but instead focused on verifiable cultural manifestations of life experience. Interpretation in the humanities still aimed at reconstructing others' insights into reality, but researchers now examined texts and documents from the past to map the social–historical world, or what Dilthey called the 'objective spirit' of any given cultural period. The idea was to gather from a variety of contemporary documents—such as historical accounts, sermons, official state or church registries, artwork, and literary texts—enough overlapping information to determine a collective social vision of a particular period. According to Dilthey, the interpreter translates the objectifications of life from documents back into the spiritual life from which they emerge.

For example, if a historian wants to understand the 19th-century Prussian statesman, Otto von Bismarck, he cannot simply regard this remarkable figure abstractly as unique genius but has to reconstruct him as a product of Prussian society at the time. Bismarck is the 'intersection' (*Kreuzungspunkt*) of that particular period's spirit as expressed in the governmental, legislative, and religious expressions of Prussia. By studying these life expressions as the empirical evidence of the human spirit, the interpreter is able to *re-experience* the collective outlook of a bygone world, even if this world is no longer her own. The reader now *understands* the objective spirit of 19th-century Prussian society, how Bismarck was shaped by it and how he shaped it in turn. Unlike Schleiermacher, Dilthey attempted to enter into not merely an individual mind but into the collective or 'objective' cultural spirit of a historical period. What else is gained from this laborious interpretive process? By understanding past societies, we gain insight into human nature and thus self-understanding, a better sense of who we are as human beings.

We don't do history; we are history

Dilthey liked to say that only history can tell us what we are as human beings. With this statement, he affirmed two important hermeneutic insights. First, self-understanding is possible only indirectly through the hermeneutic detour of interpreting life expressions from others. We only know what being human means and how to evaluate ourselves by studying other people and cultures. Second, Dilthey's hermeneutics marks the first truly historical turn in our conversation about knowledge. In Schleiermacher, we were connected to others' minds and the past through the world-Spirit. In Dilthey, by contrast, past and present experiences of life are connected through the stream of history in which we all stand. He believed that understanding others and ourselves is possible because we are beings who have made history and know ourselves only through this history.

This historicity of our existence is both the condition of, but also the limit to, our self-understanding. We can know what we are by studying the past expressions of life experience in texts, monuments, and cultural artefacts. We will not, however, find in them any fixed template of what it means to be human. Who we are is an open-ended question in the humanities. According to Dilthey, the totality of our human nature is only history. Let's say, for example, we want to assert our human dignity. We can't just take the idea of human dignity from some timeless storage room of ideas and look at it. Rather, we have access to the meaning of human dignity through the long historical development of this idea. Knowing this history gives us a much needed perspective to engage critically the impacts on human identity by genetic science, for example. The point is that we don't *do* history, as if the past was like an object we can handle. For Dilthey, we *are* history, insofar as our self-understanding requires the constant recovery and appropriation of our past cultural heritage, the mediation of past and present. Dilthey is thus one of the first hermeneutic thinkers to express the historical nature of human consciousness.

Husserl's phenomenology

Descartes had left philosophy with a gap between mind and world, leaving us with the question of how thought could be reconciled with reality. Modern epistemology thus focused on the problem of verification. True knowledge is what a disembodied human mind verifies based on rational principles. Thus, modern epistemology views the world as an assemblage of naked objects our minds then endow with some kind of meaning. But what if objects have intrinsic meaning in the way that they appear to us? What if there is no split between the mind and the world? What if the world and our consciousness are correlated in such a way that what appears to the mind, contrary to Descartes, really puts us in touch with the real nature of the object itself?

Edmund Husserl (1859–1938) is credited with the insight that objects always appear to human consciousness *as* endowed with meaning. For example, I do not have some kind of undistinguished sense experience that I subsequently interpret as an apple. My immediate experience is that of an apple itself. That human perception is always a 'seeing as' was the cardinal insight of what Husserl called *phenomenology*, a rigorous philosophical description of how phenomena (i.e. anything from a mailbox to an imagined fairy) disclose themselves to us in their meaning. Husserl's philosophical battle cry was 'to the things themselves'.

For example, when we see an apple, whether with our eyes or in our memory, Husserl believed that we really are in touch with the essence or true meaning of apple. This is so because the mind as part of reality is not a self-enclosed sphere but essentially correlated with objects in the world. For Husserl, the task of philosophy was now to study how objects revealed themselves in their immediate relation to the observer. Husserl's phenomenology was a big step beyond modern epistemology, but he retained human consciousness as the starting point of philosophy. It remained for his student Heidegger to challenge this foundation of modern epistemology.

Martin Heidegger: to be human is to interpret

The German philosopher Martin Heidegger (1889–1976) once said that Husserl's phenomenology 'gave me the eyes to see'. Husserl had shown him how to close the gap between mind and world—well, almost. For Heidegger, Husserl's link between mind and perceived objects relied still too much on Descartes's inner world of the mind. Heidegger argued that objects in the world disclosed their meaning not merely conceptually to our minds, but through our practical relation to them in daily life. With Heidegger, our conversation about knowledge moves most fully from epistemology to ontology, that is, from theories about knowledge to the life context that provides the conditions for knowledge in the first place. The story is told about a fisherman who kept throwing large fish back into the river and kept only the puny ones. Asked by an exasperated onlooker what he was doing, the angler replied: 'I only have a 10 inch frying pan'. For Heidegger, modern epistemology is like this frying pan which is incapable of holding the larger truths of human life that are often captured in literature, poetry, theology, and art.

Heidegger argued that hermeneutics is not a theory of interpretive principles but a philosophical analysis of the way we move about in the world. Heidegger gave Dilthey's claim that we are historical beings its full hermeneutical weight. We don't *do* hermeneutics; we *are* self-interpreting animals, beings whose very nature is to negotiate a complex world of meaning relations into which we are thrown at birth. We are born into families, cities and nations, languages, institutions, ideas, and social values that shape our understanding of the world. Even more profoundly, the meaning of our lives is determined by birth and death, by our fears, moods, and desires. Within this matrix of meaningful relations, we are constantly interpreting and being interpreted, told who we are but also coming to understand ourselves and trying to realize the future possibilities for our lives.

Understanding is now no longer something we come to possess after a conscious interpretive effort. This is still how Schleiermacher and Dilthey had used the term. For Heidegger, by contrast, understanding is what we unconsciously do every day by conducting ourselves, more or less skilfully, in the totality of meaningful relations that make up our world. To be human is to interpret. The task of hermeneutics as a philosophical discipline, at least for the early Heidegger, is to make visible the meaning structures within which we exist as interpreting animals. He called these structures 'existentials' (*Existentialien*) because they determine at the deepest ontological level how we perceive the world.

For this hermeneutic effort, the scientific posture of examining an object from a distance is completely useless, because such a stance catapults the interpreter out of the very life relations he needs to probe. Instead, the interpreter has to be completely engaged and try to make transparent the very structures of being he himself inhabits.

Heidegger's 'world'

A good point of entry into Heidegger's hermeneutics is to consider what we mean when we say 'world'. Modern epistemology thinks of world as an assemblage of objects at which we look. Let's call that a *theoretical stance* towards the world. Heidegger suggested that the 'world' is less like a science laboratory in which we observe things in a detached way and more like a home with which we are familiar. Let's call this an *existential stance* within the world. When we are at home, our lives are determined by the projects we are engaged in. We want to vacuum the house, wash the car, hang up a picture, or host a friend for dinner. Living in light of projects characterizes our being in the world as future-directed. This future directedness expresses itself in the ontological structure of 'attentiveness' (*Besorgnis*). Attentiveness means we relate to things around us with an eye to how they assist us in completing the tasks we are striving to accomplish.

Heidegger's hammer

Heidegger's famous example for this existential mode of being in the world is the use of a hammer. Engaged in the project of hanging up a picture, we reach for a hammer. We do not perceive the hammer as an examinable object, but as part of our project, as a means that is ready to hand (*zuhanden*) so that we have the complementary German word to 'vorhanden' below. In Heidegger's jargon, our normal relation to things has the ontological structure of 'in-order-to' (*um-zu*). Only when the hammer's head flies off the handle—or something similar interrupts our intentional activity—do we take up a theoretical stance and examine the hammer's composition. The hammer is now present as an abstract object (*vorhanden*). This abstraction from life, however necessary at times, is not our primary way of perceiving things. Rather, the being of something, whether it is a hammer, an idea, or the meaning of a text, is disclosed not to the detached or abstract analytical gaze but emerges in the context of our engaging it within a meaningful life context.

The existential hermeneutic circle

Heidegger's hammer illustrates his deepening of the hermeneutic circle to the universal existential dimensions of life: the common human project we all seek to complete is life with its future possibilities. The 'in-order-to' structure of our life projects is 'care'. Our being in the world and our relation to things are united into a meaningful whole through our will and desire to realize our future possibilities in accomplishing our life as a task. This task is framed naturally as the meaningful whole between birth and death.

Human life is thus an essentially interpretive enterprise, a continual future oriented movement of self-understanding within which we interpret texts, life situations, and other things. We are thrown into this hermeneutic circle by birth, and the cultural traditions in which our outlook is formed provide us with a certain pre-understanding about the things we encounter in the world. Language, concepts, and cultural traditions shape our perception of life.

For Heidegger, language is really the means by which we have a world in the first place—it is *the most* important medium for relating to the world. Particularly for the later Heidegger, language is what makes the world a home to us, providing the symbolic web of meaning relations that make up the conceptual map by which we interpret the world. His claims that 'Language is the house of being', or that 'Language speaks us' are provocative phrases meant to indicate that language is not a tool to name objects in the world but the very lens through which we understand the world and ourselves. The crucial point is that such pre-understanding, as conveyed through language and tradition, is not a prison or anything negative from which we have to disengage. On the contrary, it is what makes our meaningful engagement of the world possible in the first place. Of course, we don't stay with the received meaning, as if we were slaves to tradition. Driven by our desire to achieve the task of life, our understanding creatively appropriates and reshapes the received preconceptions.

Hermeneutics after Heidegger

Heidegger moved the hermeneutic conversation about knowledge firmly onto the ontological plane. Understanding is once again inseparably linked to our experience of life and our being in the world. The gulf between mind and world is not merely bridged but abolished as an unnatural distortion of human perception. After Heidegger, hermeneutics is determined by two basic insights. First, pre-understanding or preconceptions are deemed an essential, intrinsic part of interpretation. Any pretensions to presuppositionless interpretation, of approaching texts or whatever it is we interpret without bias, must be given up. The Enlightenment ideal of reading without prejudice, formulated by Descartes, Kant, and others, is not just undesirable but impossible, since access to whatever we want to interpret is only granted through presuppositions.

Heidegger's second insight is that the reason we can engage the world meaningfully is the temporal, historical nature of our being. History is not a barrier but the very thing connecting us to the cultural traditions that are giving us the initial lenses through which we see the world. But this is not fate. When Heidegger said that history 'sends' us the questions we have to wrestle with, he asserted our freedom to appropriate creatively our cultural heritage in light of our own present situation. Hermeneutics after Heidegger is thus much more than the claim that everyone comes to interpretation from a certain perspective. The universal claim of hermeneutics is rather that interpretation is a human condition. Hermeneutics describes the common human endeavour to interpret past traditions in light of pressing contemporary questions in order to make future oriented decisions for completing the project that is our life.

Chapter 3
Philosophical hermeneutics

Philosophical hermeneutics refers to the detailed and systematic examination of human understanding that began with the German philosopher Hans-Georg Gadamer (1900–2002). In a famous book entitled *Truth and Method*, Gadamer drew together many of the previously discussed insights from Schleiermacher, Dilthey, Husserl, and Heidegger to provide an extensive description of what understanding is.

We should note that Gadamer entitled his book 'Truth *and* Method', not 'Truth *or* Method'. To be sure, the book is a massive defence of the humanities and the kind of truth pursued in the liberal arts, but Gadamer did not simply oppose moral insight in the human sciences to method-driven knowledge in the natural sciences. Rather, he recognized the importance of methodical procedures for obtaining knowledge. As did his teacher, Heidegger, Gadamer argued, however, that the event of understanding something, whether this occurs in the natural or the human sciences, cannot be reduced to methodology. With Heidegger, Gadamer believed that our perception of the world is not primarily theoretical but practical. We don't assess objects neutrally from a distance, but they disclose themselves to us as we move around in an already existing totality of meaningful relations. Consequently, Gadamer did not view understanding as one possible attitude we adopt in relating to the world. Rather, following Heidegger, he regarded understanding as the basic movement of human existence that encompasses the whole of life experience.

Gadamer developed Heidegger's hermeneutics further by applying his teacher's insights to the aesthetic experience of art and literature. In the same way that Heidegger probed the ontological structures of being-in-the-world, Gadamer attempted to describe our relation to art and texts. According to him, our experience of art is exemplary for what happens to us generally when we understand anything at all. How do we experience truth through artistic creations? In what way is it possible for a text, play, symphony, or painting to impart real knowledge about ourselves and our world? These are the questions Gadamer used to unfold the nature of human understanding.

Historically effected consciousness

Gadamer followed Dilthey and Heidegger by making the historical character of human life foundational to understanding. Husserl, Dilthey, and Heidegger had rejected the flawed modern concept of objectivity, according to which a mind disengaged from history and sense experience examines the world dispassionately. Gadamer agreed that this gulf between mind and world leads to the wrong idea of knowledge as the possession of facts about an object and to an obsession with method for arriving at verifiable knowledge. Following Heidegger, Gadamer argued that we obtain objective understanding about anything only by allowing an object to disclose itself through the meaningful relations within which it appears to us. Gadamer's idea of objective knowledge is closer to the ancient view discussed at the beginning of Chapter 2. Knowledge is not something that we acquire and control as a possession but something in which we already participate. The reason we understand anything at all is because we already stand *in* it.

Take history, for example. It seems natural for us moderns to look at the past across a great chasm of time, as if we stood at one side of the Grand Canyon with, let's say, the events of the French Revolution unfolding on the opposite side, separated from us by a great gulf of time. But do we really direct our gaze at historical events across a chasm of time, examining them as objects disconnected from our own viewpoint? This experience of distance, which Gadamer called our 'historical consciousness', correctly registers the differences between cultural periods. Yet we forget that just as the deep valley that separates the rims of the Grand Canyon also connects them, so do time itself and our nature as historical beings, connect us to the past. The past is not 'out there' presenting us with objects to examine. Rather, history is like a stream in which we move and participate in every act of understanding. The very reason that we can understand anything at all from the past is because we already stand in the stream of time that connects past and present.

To return to our example, the French Revolution has meaning for us because the historical effects of this event are still very much operative within culture, and determine the way we talk about freedom, solidarity, and human rights. Since history itself is not a barrier to understanding but the actual ground that makes it possible, Gadamer suggested we should not talk about our consciousness *of* history but about our *historically effected consciousness*, that is, about the way our very awareness of the world comes about because of history and its formative effect on how we perceive things.

The conversation that we are

Like Heidegger, Gadamer was convinced that the formative effects of history that shape our understanding of the world work primarily through language. After we are born into a culture, we are gradually inducted into its outlook by absorbing the ideas and concepts residing in language. From childhood, we learn to orient ourselves in the world by associating objects and situations with words and signs. In short, we have a meaningful world only through language. The meaningful totality of this symbolic universe always precedes us so that learning a language and getting to know our world are really the same thing. Gadamer claimed that as fish swim in water, so we move in language—our consciousness of the world and our thoughts move within its matrix. It is through language that we have a common, truly human world across time and across cultures.

The modern ideal of knowledge started with a self disengaged from the world, imagining itself as observing and reaching out to the world. This division of the knowing subject from its objects of knowledge is fundamentally mistaken if the historically formed self inhabits a meaningful world through language. For Gadamer, language is the medium in which mind and world are always already connected, and it is this very connection that provides the ground for objective knowledge. By being born into and moving about in the world of language, the self participates in something greater than itself, ruling out subjectivism from the start.

Languages have developed over millennia in correspondence with reality and thus disclose our objective understanding of a shared world. Language is objective because it is ordered to the world rather than to our subjective consciousness. We don't make up language; we come to its objective reality. Language guarantees the objectivity of our thought, because, as Gadamer once put it, there is no 'first word'—we never think in isolation, but use inherited conceptual vocabulary and step into an already existing conversation regardless of the topic, often one that stretches across millennia. To capture the sense that our understanding of ourselves and our world depends on language and our participation in ongoing discussions of perennial human questions, Gadamer described us as 'the conversation that we are'.

At the same time, we should not think of the symbolic web in which we live as the limitation of a prison. While there is never a first word insofar as we enter into an existing conversation, equipped with an already existing language and inherited outlook, the 'conversation that we are' also includes our human freedom for *changing* the conversation. We are beings who think in language, and we think in the language of tradition, not as parrots, but as *artists* who creatively appropriate and reshape inherited questions and answers about what it means to be human.

Take the word 'person', for example, which crops up all the time in political discussions about human dignity and personal rights. We simply assume that a person has dignity and should be accorded rights, but when we go back to the Latin origins of the term, we find that *persona* has a merely functional meaning, designating an actor's role in a play, or someone's role in society. It is only through many complicated and important historical developments that a 'person' became the full-blooded, dignified being we associate with this term today. Knowing the history of the word 'person' thus helps us to understand better who we are. Even more importantly, however, the history of concepts shows us that their meanings are not simply given but have developed over time and can therefore change. The point is that important insights or values can be attained and lost again. According to Gadamer, it is the task of the humanities to act as cultural memory by keeping the history of concepts alive and by guarding important insights for future generations.

Tradition and authority are good things!

Gadamer believed that recognizing the importance of history and language for our perception of the world would renew our appreciation for the role tradition and authority play in understanding. During the 17th and 18th centuries, many philosophers believed that only by freeing thought from the blinders of tradition and authority could the searchlight of critical reason illumine the darkness of religious superstitions and outmoded ways of thinking. During this cultural period we now call 'The Enlightenment', tradition and authority became the enemy of reason or critical thought. The modern ideal of knowledge has left us with a kind of teenage mentality toward authority and tradition as inherently bad because they shackle our freedom of self-expression and independent thought: what parents tell us must be wrong because they are obviously conservative and biased, dead set against our autonomy.

Perhaps this modern ideal of knowledge surfaces most clearly in the phrase, 'let me make up my own mind'. Do we really, literally, 'make up' our minds as if we were filling a blank slate with carefully selected knowledge? There is, of course, nothing wrong with wanting to think *for* oneself, as long as we don't fall prey to the illusion that we could actually think *by* ourselves, in isolation from the traditions and authorities that guide our thinking.

Gadamer showed why this prejudice against guiding influences was mistaken. For him, tradition and authority are not the enemy of reason or critical thought. Rather, tradition furnishes the web of conceptions within which we live, move, and have our historical being. To be sure, as we all know, tradition and authority can and often are abused, but such distortions should not mislead us into denying their important role for our perception of the world. Authority, for example, is ideally never imposed but derives from the superior skill or life-experience we recognize in others. The now perhaps slightly quaint expression that someone is 'an authority on ancient languages' reminds us that authority derives from someone's mastery of a subject. Indeed, authority and tradition are linked precisely in the recognition that our knowledge about the world depends on others who have mastered and passed on skills accumulated by tradition.

This positive view of tradition as the storehouse of human knowledge recognizes the natural limits of human finitude. No individual can reinvent from scratch insights gained over many generations, but rather always draws on the handed-down experience of tradition through recognized authorities. It is no accident that the word 'tradition' comes from the Latin 'tradere', meaning, 'to hand over'. We always already move within a tradition and implicitly appeal to authority—the authority of scientific evidence or legal precedent, for example. Denying this will only make us blind to the influences that do impact our understanding. The goal is to become aware of these guiding influences and creatively adopt those that are fruitful while weeding out those that cripple our thinking.

Seeing or hearing?

If indeed our historical being-in-the-world is like a conversation, then the way we come to understand things is more like a dialogue with interested people than a scientific investigation. Understanding this world therefore requires an attentive ear. We need to become sensitive to the development of concepts that shape our understanding of the world. We must hear the question to which such ideas or concepts are the answer. For philosophical hermeneutics, every text that we encounter is essentially an answer to a previously asked question. For that matter, every idea or concept that has developed over time is a response to a question. What is justice? How do we define freedom? What is the nature of the cosmos? Scientific texts, histories, plays, novels, legal dispositions, and philosophical discourses are answers to questions that in turn pose new questions that require new responses. How a question is asked in part determines the answer, and latecomers to a conversation can often see more clearly the limitations of an earlier answer and provide a better one. Of course, given the richness of life and the natural limits of human reason, answers are rarely final. Especially when we deal with concepts and ideas, each answer or definition only discloses part of the whole truth.

We don't often think about the dialogical nature of understanding because we often employ the metaphor of sight. 'I see what you

3. Questioning vision as a metaphor for knowing.

mean', or 'let me see if I understand', and similar expressions indicate our preference for such metaphors. Sometimes when philosophers defend hermeneutics against the charge of relativism, they similarly resort to the popular Indian tale about the subjective nature of truth (see Figure 3). We all know the story: six blind men are standing around an elephant, each taking hold of a different part and trying to define this thing called 'elephant'. Each grasps only a partial truth of the object before them, and yet we know they are all dealing with the same objectively present thing under investigation.

This story is sometimes used to illustrate the hermeneutic claim that our interpretations do get at the real object but only reveal a certain part of the whole. The immediate problem with this illustration, however, is that partial understanding is presented as deficiency. The men are *blind*. Presumably, if they were healed, their sight would grant them immediate access to the whole elephant; yet according to hermeneutic philosophy, as finite human beings, we only ever have partial access to an object. Another problem is the illustration's implicit appeal to someone who actually does see the elephant in its entirety and can assure us that each blind man's partial impression is indeed connected to the whole. To whom or what do we appeal for this total vision?

At the very least, the elephant illustration demonstrates the importance of word-pictures and how such metaphors are built into our understanding of reality. It matters deeply how we picture our access to truth. Do we expect to 'see' immediately or do we seek understanding through the process of a conversation that requires patient listening and attention to the meaning of words? Do we compare understanding to the primarily impersonal experience of observation or to the intrinsically relational, interpersonal experience of conversation? Do we see or do we hear? For Gadamer, at least, hearing is a superior metaphor to seeing in describing the hermeneutic nature of our being in the world. The notion of listening to a conversation more adequately conveys how we come to know and negotiate the world through language and tradition. For him, every meaningful interaction with the world occurs through language, a sentiment captured in his well-known adage, 'being that can be understood is language'.

The heart of hermeneutic experience: mediation

For Gadamer, understanding works essentially as *mediation*. Mediation is the heart of hermeneutic experience. What does he mean by mediation? The reader may be familiar with this term from conflict resolution. For example, when talks between striking workers and an employer break down, they call in a mediator who moves between the two camps to reconcile their differences and unite them in a common agreement. Reaching such an agreement usually requires concessions from each party so that the original position taken by each side changes. Gadamer believed that learning through understanding involved a similar kind of mediation. We perform this mediating or integrating work of understanding constantly as we encounter new situations in our lives. Even in popular parlance, we call this expansion the broadening of our horizons, for example when we encounter new things while travelling to foreign places. When we understand, we unite our own perspective with another's viewpoint into a greater unifying context, and this experience transforms us by expanding our own perspective on things.

Gadamer credited the German philosopher G. W. F. Hegel (1770–1831) with the realization that this transformative act of mediation is not limited to moments of conflict or misunderstanding, because integrating the alien and the familiar forms the basic structure of human experience. Experience is not merely the encounter with something unforeseen but always includes our being changed by this encounter. We learn when we confront something unfamiliar and integrate it into what we already know. Hermeneutic philosophers have wondered what the enabling conditions for this integration are. Why is it that the strange does not simply remain strange and inaccessible to us? How can we engage and gain access to what confronts us as different in the first place? The answer lies in the human ability to detect similarity in difference. When we encounter something unfamiliar, we engage it by relating it to what is already familiar to us.

Integrating the strange into the familiar, however, does not merely assimilate the new element into our own frame of reference, but also changes our own mental horizon. The French post-modern philosopher Jacques Derrida (1930–2004), who argued for truth as something never settled and always disruptive, missed this important point. Derrida worried that hermeneutics blunts the disruptive power of truth by forcing it to conform to the interpreter's mental horizon. Derrida overlooked, however, Gadamer's insistence that we have to expand our initial outlook to accommodate a new insight. Since understanding is fundamentally the mediation between the alien and the familiar leading to a new, enlarged perspective, Gadamer could say that hermeneutic experience is best described as education. He used the German equivalent word *Bildung*, which means literally the shaping or cultivating of the human spirit.

Fusion of horizons

The same mediation of the alien and the familiar occurs when we read texts from the past. When we read an ancient philosophical text or one of Shakespeare's plays, we encounter a world that is different from ours. And yet, the texts seem to speak to us, and contain much that seems familiar. In fact, these familiar aspects draw us into their orbits and hold our attention.

Imagine, for example, that someone who has had a brush with cancer reads Socrates' famous *Apology* mentioned earlier in Chapter 1. In the *Apology*, Socrates justified his life before the tribunal that would sentence him to death unfairly for political reasons. The modern reader's outlook is likely shaped by our culture's view of death as something to be feared and postponed as long as possible in order to enjoy the pleasures of life. Yet in Socrates' apology, he meets with a strangely different view. The modern idea of prolonging life and seeking happiness in consumerist pleasures crippled rather than enhanced a blessed life for Socrates. Instead, Socrates presented the satisfaction that comes from a well-examined life oriented toward virtue as not only the highest personal aspiration but also as the very foundation of a healthy society.

Clearly, Socrates' outlook was formed within a different world, a world without cancer treatments, without the advanced medical knowledge and technology that prolong our lives today, raising even visions of genetic enhancements that may reverse ageing altogether. In addition, Socrates' courage in the face of death may also have been bolstered by his belief in a 'deathless soul' many moderns no longer share. Nonetheless, the modern reader is impacted by Socrates' view: could it be that the modern attitude toward ageing and death has serious negative consequences for how we understand happiness? Do we tend to avoid the visible signs of suffering and death, instead of embracing them as part of the human condition? Could this attitude, especially in a consumerist society, prompt us to devalue old and handicapped people as unproductive burdens rather than as resources of life experience? Should our modern society, while rightly pursuing medical improvements, become more aware of how such changes alter our values and perhaps think of some countermeasures to these alterations?

What we are observing in our modern reader is the process Gadamer called 'fusion of horizons'. While there is much that is unfamiliar in the ancient outlook the reader encounters, Socrates' voice from the past horizon still speaks to the reader. What connects these two horizons? For one, the common, human, hermeneutic universe, which is full of artistic and literary ruminations about death, provides a connection. Moreover, having grown up in a Western context, our reader will likely have some inkling about who Socrates is as well as recognize that the Platonic dialogues are part of our cultural heritage. Indeed, the fact alone that most medical expressions still derive from Greek or Latin roots (e.g. *antibiotics*—that which destroys the life of bacteria) even reminds us that as modern readers of ancient texts, we move within a certain cultural–linguistic context, within a certain cultural tradition, that connects past and present.

Tradition, as Gadamer told us before, is thus not a hindrance to understanding but the foundation that makes it possible. Understanding is to be thought of less as subjective, isolated act of consciousness than as participating in an event of tradition, a process of transmission in which past and present are constantly mediated. Since we already stand within the stream of history with its traditions, our existence is constituted by the mediation of the past and present, and this conversation becomes a conscious dialogue whenever past concepts or texts speak to us.

As we have seen, the modern reader also brings to the text cultural assumptions about the topic of interest. These preconceptions are often held unconsciously but they generate our interest in the text in the first place. The moment our reader picks up Socrates' *Apology*, he tries to grasp what the text is about as a whole. His mind makes a prejudgement based on what he knows about philosophy, about Socrates, and what he assumes about mortality. Yet as he reads line by line, and learns more about what Socrates actually says about life, the reader's initial preconception about the text will change. According to Gadamer, the reader would ideally begin reading such a text with the best understanding possible of its content and context. Once again, we meet here with the famous *hermeneutic circle*, the movement between parts and the whole that is also operative in unifying horizons from the past and the present. The outcome of uniting past and present horizons, of this 'fusion', is the transformation of the reader.

The soul of hermeneutic experience: application

If mediation as the central movement of understanding is the heart of hermeneutic experience, then *application* is its motivating power, its soul. In the previous example, the reader relates to Socrates because of his personal need to reflect on mortality. Is it not true that we only really engage a text or another's viewpoint when we want to know what meaning another's perspective has *for us*? It is the hope of every teacher that students in reading an assigned text will begin to see its relevance for their own lives. If this does not happen, the text will remain a foreign object without meaning. For Gadamer, application motivates engaged reading and set in motion the mediation of another perspective with one's own.

We recall that the modern ideal of knowledge asserted that disengaged observation without any kind of personal interest guaranteed objective knowledge. Philosophical hermeneutics takes the exact opposite view. Personal interest in what something means for me in my particular life situation makes understanding possible in the first place. The ancient philosopher Aristotle showed the importance of personal application in moral reasoning. Abstract knowledge of ethical principles does not constitute actual knowledge until I am forced to apply it in a concrete situation. Only through their actual use in a concrete life situation do I come to know the meaning and truth of moral precepts, because it is only in their enactment that they gain real-life significance. Theological and legal hermeneutics are exemplary for this applicatory aspect of interpretation. The believer opens the sacred text to hear what God has to say to him today. Likewise, the judge studies the law and legal precedents in light of a concrete case.

For Gadamer, application was thus essential to understanding. If all interpretations are necessarily motivated by personal interest, however, are we not already on the feared slippery slope to subjectivism? Indeed, Gadamer himself seemed to feed this anxiety when he argued that 'each interpreter understands the work differently'. Is not this a clear admission that I can impose my subjective fancies on the text? No it is not. Gadamer's point is that any understanding, whether of a text or another's utterance, requires that I pull the other's statement into the concrete orbit of my own circumstances. And since these circumstances are always different, interpretation cannot proceed simply by templates or rules. The very idea of a text's relevance requires my reading it in light of present concerns.

The task of hermeneutics, however, is not to gloss over the tension between the past and present horizon, but to become fully aware of it. Thus, a careful interpreter performs the necessary historical-critical work of establishing the author's view as expressed within a different socio-cultural environment. At this level, methodical work and interpretive rules find their rightful place. Yet the interpreter performs even this necessary historical work with his inner ear attuned to the demands of the present. (Remember, hearing is better than seeing!) For this reason, texts, and especially literary texts, cannot be reduced to one single moral message. This is true even for a great literary or philosophical text read by the same interpreter over the course of her life; as her own mental horizon shifts and develops, the same text speaks differently. This is not to say that only certain aspects of the text speak at any given time while others remain silent, though this may also happen. Rather, given my own shifting horizon in the present, the text as a whole illuminates my life differently depending on the concrete life situation from which I pose my questions to the text. Therefore, to say that there is not one final correct interpretation of a text is not to deny the possibility of misinterpretation but to remain faithful to the dynamic movement of understanding that characterizes human life itself.

Beyond objectivism and relativism

We have come to see that the hermeneutic ideal of knowledge differs from modern epistemology. Not distance but involvement, not impersonal observation but personal interaction, not thinking against prejudice or tradition but accessing knowledge through them, characterizes our perception of the world. For Gadamer, this engaged knowing was not relativism because how we come to know things is not akin to working in a science laboratory but rather more like playing a game. The dynamic of a game is analogous to how we interpret and demonstrates how subjective and objective aspects work together. When playing a game, we need to get involved and lose ourselves. In doing so, we enter into a pre-existing, objective structure we cannot change at will lest we spoil the game; but within its rules, we have freedom to play. In fact, the game only comes alive through the players. The dynamics of a game thus go beyond the options of relativist subjectivism on the one hand, and cold, disengaged objectivity on the other. As we had already seen in Chapter 1, true objectivity requires the engagement of the knower.

Gadamer argued that the knowledge we derive from art operates precisely in this way. Like a game, art draws us into its orbit, but a text or play only comes alive through the interpretive work of the reader or actor. Only by engaging a game, practice, or research object, only by being involved can I understand. The old scientific objectivism was wrong, therefore, to speak of detached knowing. At the same time, this involvement has nothing to do with relativism. It does not, because the reader cannot simply make up meaning but has to enter into the text's or play's *given structure*—this is the passive aspect of interpretation—even while the reader also plays an active role in performing the mediating work of interpretation we described as a fusion of horizons. This work happens whether a reader 'performs' a text within her imagination when reading, or witnesses it on a stage.

The power of art

Indeed, the activity of performance best suggests the power of art to convey knowledge about life. The modern ideal of knowledge sidelined art, along with religion and moral philosophy, dismissing it as unverifiable subjective knowledge. Art may have the power to move us emotionally, or it may serve as an escape from the constantly shifting demands of reality; art may even provide pleasure through depicting purely formal visions of timeless beauty, but it does not provide knowledge about reality. Philosophical hermeneutics, by contrast, insists that art possesses the power to convey true knowledge about our human condition. And this power is best described as creative performance. In Chapter 1 we said that hermeneutics is the art of understanding but also of making oneself understood. Both aspects play an important part in how art conveys truth.

First, the hermeneutic aspect of making oneself understood plays an important role in artistic creation. In a first creative performance, an author, playwright, painter or sculptor captures aspects of human life and draws them together into the whole of a novel, a play, a statue, or even a historical account of the past. Created in order to be displayed, read, or performed, artwork is the most conscious expression of what human understanding always entails: the interpretive integration of life's details into a meaningful whole. The author's creation is therefore already an act of interpretation in which an impression about life is joined with the most congenial literary or artistic form of expressing the artist's take on human reality. In this activity, neither artistic material, such as paint, canvas, marble, or clay, nor stylistic forms, such as word pictures and poetic structures, are arbitrary choices. The artist will intuitively choose the artistic medium that is most suitable for expressing the intended meaning. Only form and content together convey truth. To return to our example of *Othello*: the play captures the debilitating dynamics of jealousy in dramatic form, thus giving concrete expression to the character of jealousy as a 'green-eyed monster', able to extinguish any compassion. As Othello puts it, 'No, my heart is turned to stone; I strike it, and it hurts my hand.' Interpretation, in other words, is always a form of ordering the fragments of our impressions into a coherent presentation.

Understanding this original presentation by the artist requires a second performative re-presentation in which a text or play is brought alive and carried into the present. The director and actors in a play only do more visibly what is every reader's interpretive act of making present again the insights about life an author had captured in his text. Given the depth and complexity of life experience, no single re-presenting interpretation can possibly capture every aspect of an author's composition. Every faithful interpretation of a text does, however, reveal a partial vision of what the work is about. It is for this reason that a reader should always pay careful attention to the history of faithful interpretations to gain a more informed, if not exhaustive, sense of a work's possible range of meanings.

Philosophical hermeneutics thus rehabilitates the power of art to convey real knowledge about ourselves. Art helps us understand ourselves better and thus make more intelligent decisions about life. Art helps us to identify and understand previously invisible forces that shape our lives and thus to deal with them. In what is perhaps its greatest gift to us, art makes possible *recognition*, the power allowing us to say, 'Yes, that's how it is, now I understand.'

Chapter 4
Hermeneutics and the humanities

Texting

Many complain that our current mobile-phone culture replaces living conversations with text messages. This change, they say, teaches us to avoid personal interaction through spoken dialogue and flattens language to express only banalities through texting (see Figure 4). These worries are well founded, but texting reminds us, even if in an absurd way, of the hermeneutic claim that our understanding of the world emerges through conversation with others, and that textual communication is an important part of this process.

The texting craze on tablets and mobile phones also highlights for us the difference between spoken and written conversation. In a face to face conversation, not only do we have another's body language to help us grasp what is being said, but we also have recourse to another's living presence to clarify meaning. An email or tweet, by contrast, is more easily misunderstood because it has been detached from this living context. Yet this very detachment also allows the text to become, in a sense, timeless. Not only will the text live beyond its moment of creation, but it will also become universally transmittable and accessible to all who can read. Twitter in particular demonstrates powerfully the universality texts possess for communicating ideas.

4. **Texting gone wrong.**

In a sense, 'texting' is also the main occupation of knowledge disciplines we call 'the humanities'. Texting in the humanities, of course demands a longer attention span and involves complex ideas. Nevertheless, theology, philosophy, law, history, and literary studies deal mainly with the transmission and interpretation of texts. The technical term for textual interpretation in the humanities is 'exegesis': an explanation of important texts, often from past cultures and written in ancient languages, that require careful reconstruction, explanation, and commentary. The need for historical-critical exegesis, the work of reconstructing a text in its original social-historical context, demonstrates the special challenge posed by written communications from the past: we have to make these texts speak again before we can hear what they have to say

58

For example, when in Shakespear's *Hamlet*, the courtier Laertes tells his sister Ophelia, 'O, fear me not', he doesn't tell her not to be afraid of him. The modern reader has to do some work to grasp the older meaning of 'do not fret about me'—in other words, don't worry about me. The social conventions and archaic language of Shakespeare are roughly 400 years old, while other texts, such as the Bible or Plato's dialogues, are much older and require careful attention to linguistic and cultural differences. This philological work remains important because these texts are the carriers of enduring cultural values and insights into the perennial questions about who we are and how we should live.

Getting it right: the validity of interpretations

Most scholars in the humanities agree that reading is always an interpretive act by which we seek to understand what the text says to us. The hermeneutic philosopher Paul Ricoeur (1913–2005) once helpfully remarked that the interpretation of texts follows the same basic structure of any human communication: someone is saying something about something to someone else. As stated in Chapter 1, interpretation of texts is the effort to understand what someone is saying to me about something. Reading texts, however, is not exactly the same as having a face to face conversation. Without the author's living presence, his body language and gestures, we have to rely on his thoughts as expressed in writing. Without the author's presence, how do we know whether we have interpreted something correctly? How can we distinguish between valid and invalid intepretations? Is there only one correct interpretation? If not, then how do we adjudicate between conflicting interpretations? Hermeneutic thinkers have dealt with such questions about the validity of interpretation in essentially two ways.

Hirsch's hermeneutic objectivism

The first solution is motivated by the fear of relativism: how do we avoid subjective interpretation that turns the text into a mirror of our own views? This was the overriding concern of the American educator and literary critic, E. D. Hirsch (1928–), who targeted four groups of interpreters who opened the door to relativism. The first group is comprised of empathic interpreters, for whom interpretation is ultimately about recognizing another person's spirit behind the text. Hirsch rejected this kind of psychologizing interpretation that began with Schleiermacher's Romantic ideal of understanding as communion with another's soul.

New Criticism makes up the second group of subjective interpreters Hirsch examined. New Critics, a group of American literary critics dominating literary criticism from about 1940–70, sought to minimize the importance of authorial intent and historical context, scrutinizing the text itself by means of formal analysis. Hirsch's third target is French post-modern philosophers and critics (Roland Barthes, Michel Foucault, and Jacques Derrida), who proclaimed the 'death of the author'; a hyperbolic expression meant to point out that an author is not really fully in control of what he writes. Finally, Hirsch's fourth target is hermeneutic philosophers, such as Heidegger, Gadamer, and Ricoeur, because they do not separate stricly between 'description and evaluation', between what a text once meant and what it now means to us.

In his final word on interpretive relativism, Hirsch reduced these four targets to the two extremes of intuitionism and positivism, that is, to those who think they subjectively grasp the meaning of a text and those who construe what a texts says based on interpretive principles alone. Both extremes open the door to relativism: intuitionism because the text means whatever a reader wants it to mean, and postivism because relying on method only hides prejudices and is equally subjectivisitic. Hirsch wanted to find a middle ground between these extremes.

Hirsch's main weapon for fending off relativism was to establish the author's intended meaning as the changeless object of interpretation. He argued that the intended meaning of the original author determined the correct interpretation of texts. By using the term *original* author, Hirsch limited authorial intent to the author's intended meaning of the text at the time of the work's original composition. Thus, even when an author later changes his mind about the significance of this work, its originally intended meaning stands unaltered. The great Russian writer Leo Tolstoy, for example, ended up denouncing his masterpiece *Anna Karenina* because it did not conform to his later religious ideal of art. According to Hirsch's theory, this change of mind would not affect the original meaning of the work. For Hirsch, Tolstoy merely became the interpreter of his own writing by attributing a different significance to the unchanged originally intended meaning of the text. Hirsch used this distinction between meaning and significance to ensure that the object of interpretation is one 'universally valid' meaning. What we as readers then do with that meaning—how we apply it to our own context—constitutes the work's significance, which changes from reader to reader.

Hirsch thus clearly and neatly distinguished between our construal of a text's meaning and our understanding of this meaning. For example, the sentence 'the cat is on the mat', always means the same thing, but it can have various significances, depending on whether we like cats or deem the mat off limits for cats. In effect, the author's originally intended meaning thus stands firm as a self-identical object, in the way that the number 1, or a scientific result, is reproducable and recognizable no matter who looks at it. As was the case in scientific objectivism discussed in earlier chapters, Hirsch held that any suggested interpretation, like a scientific hypothesis, should be verified against the ideal meaning intended by the original author.

Hirsch knew, of course, that no interpretation will likely ever reach the one and only correct reading that matches authorial intent. He rightly argued that, unlike another human person, a text does not just speak to us; its meaning has to be constructed from the silent letters on the page. Moreover, such construction always involves ethical criteria that are extrinsic to the text. Reconstructing a text always requires a series of choices and preferences we cannot find in the text itself. For Hirsch, however, these choices should only influence our interpretation of the text's significance for us, not, however, its originally intended meaning. He still insisted on the regulative ideal of authorial intent to forestall the (for him) otherwise inevitable consequence of interpretive relativism.

How would Hirsch's ideal work in practice? For example, when Plato censored Homer's poetry for portraying the gods as a jealous, bickering lot, toying with humanity, or when he upbraided poets for encouraging effusive emotions unfit for statesmen, Plato brought to bear his own ethical criteria on Homer's text. This judgement is coherent and defensible given Plato's own views of what good poetry should do. Even in disagreeing with Homer's virtues, Plato still recognized, however, Homer's own original intent of writing poetry to showcase moral virtue and warn against moral flaws. In the same way, even when an author like Tolstoy judges his past creations by new-found ethical standards, he still reacts to a universally recognizable set of authorial convictions about art that shaped his own former work, and determined its universally recognizable original meaning, even if he now no longer agrees with it. In Hirsch's own words, 'the only universally valid cognition of a work of art is that which is constituted by the kind of subjective stance adopted in its creation'. This univerally valid, original authorial intended meaning is the object by which any interpretive judgement is validated.

Ricoeur's response to Hirsch

The second solution to the question of how we distinguish between conflicting interpretations comes from Paul Ricoeur, who further developed the hermeneutic philosophy introduced by Hans-Georg Gadamer. Ricoeur agreed that to know is to interpret, but he also thought that Gadamer paid too little attention to how linguistic structures both limit and facilitate the interpretation of texts. Ricoeur thus empathized with Hirsch's desire to secure objective meaning. Being a hermeneutic philosopher, however, Ricoeur rejected Hirsch's division between the explication of the text's intended meaning and our subsequent understanding of its significance. Ricoeur did agree with many of Hirsch's assumptions: interpretation involves the construal of meaning from silent letters on the page, and such construction requires ethical criteria external to the text. Ricoeur disagreed, however, with Hirsch's ground rule that the most fundamental ethical principle for interpretation is to respect the original intent of the author.

Ricoeur doubted Hirsch's claim that the author's intended meaning exists as a self-identical, universally recognizable object. For Ricoeur, Hirsch's distinction between original meaning and interpretative significance did not do justice to how we actually read texts. After all, Hirsch himself admitted that every meaning has to be constructed from the written signs on the page. According to Ricoeur, this constructive effort was not the simple uncovering of a pre-existing object. If that were so, the text would be like a corpse and the reader a pathologist conducting an autopsy, cutting out the orignally intended meaning to evaluate it.

Hirsch illustrated his claim that a text always means the same thing but has varying personal significance with the simple sentence 'the cat is on the mat'. Ricoeur pointed out, however, that this example utterly fails to account for the kind of larger texts in literature, theology, history, or philosophy we call 'a work'. Such works present us not with a straight forward situation of an animal's whereabouts but with inexhaustible worlds of human experience. Reconstructing the meaning of such complex texts requires the artful integration of details into a coherent whole through an act of the imagination based on personal experience. For Ricoeur, reconstruction was thus already a work of interpretation that depended on personal choices concerning the aims, values, and norms for determination of a text's meaning. Questions of choice and value are thus an integral part of the construction of meaning.

Ricoeur's essential point is that interpretation requires a reader's personal act of integrating textual details into a meaningful whole. In order to interpret a text, we will have to highlight some aspects and neglect others, depending on our interest. Therefore Hirsch's strict separation between description and evaluation is untrue. All construction of meaning requires choice and every choice involves ethical values. If indeed these subjective aspects are essential to our construal of meaning, then Hirsch's distinction between originally intended meaning and secondary interpretive significance is false. Ricoeur understood that Hirsch clung to the idea of authorial meaning as timeless, self-identical object because he feared interpretive relativism. This fear, argued Ricoeur, stemmed from the lingering effects of modernist epistemology that separated fact from value in order to ensure objectivity. Hirsch rightly wanted to make sure that our knowledge of a text was true to its objective content, but he wrongly identified the chimera of authorial intent as the only norm that can stem the tide of relativism. Rather, as already mentioned in Chapter 1, a careful examination of the reading process shows us that objectivity can be defined in a way that goes beyond Hirsch's narrow choice between objectivism and relativism.

Interpreting objectively

The debate between Hirsch and Ricoeur demonstrates that, of interpretive rules, communion with an author's spirit, or a self-identical timeless authorial intention, not one provides an absolute measure by which we can verify our interpretation. How then do we interpret objectively? The answer lies in redefining objectivity. The desire for the one correct meaning against which we can measure our subjective interpretations is the same desire for certain meaning identified as 'foundationalism' in Chapter 2. We had concluded that this anxiety about certainty originated with the false isolation of the mind from the world around us. To redefine objectivity, we need to focus less on ourselves and turn our attention more towards the object we seek to understand.

Let us recall our basic chain of communication: someone saying something about a certain matter to someone else. Instead of focusing on the two subjective poles of this continuum—the author's intended meaning and the reader's ability to nail down this illusive object—we focus on the two middle terms, on 'what is said' about 'a certain matter'. In each case, of course, we never arrive at a wholly conclusive statement. We can never bottle the meaning of a text, put it on the shelf, and then move on to the next work. Rather, our construction of meaning is ultimately a hypothesis, that is, a well-reasoned guess.

At the same time, however, such an educated guess is not at all a merely arbitrary conjecture. For the text in itself holds all sort of clues that provide the boundaries and possibilities for the meaning we construct. For example, an author's choice of genre limits how we read a text, and social context helps too. When we read Shakespeare's *Hamlet*, we know that we're reading not a political treatise but a play, and also a certain kind of play, a revenge tragedy, which seeks to entertain but also to emphasize the consummating power and tragic consequences of seeking vengeance. These kind of restrictions, built into the text itself, limit our construction of meaning: we cannot read this text as giving political advice or as reflecting mainly on the nature of friendship. The same interpretive dynamic is at play in the writing and reading of history. A historian, too, pieces together all available clues from sources into the most convincing narrative, and the reader of history does the same in turn with the historical text. Based on these internal clues, we can exclude some interpretations because they do not fit the internal structure of the work and the world it portrays.

Our construed meaning, however, can only ever be the most probable reading, a hypothesis that best accounts for the greatest number of facets provided by the text. There is always the possibility that a reader with greater experience, a keener eye, and a better imagination can provide a more persuasive reading that integrates more of the textual parts and clues into a convincing whole. This kind of interpretation is no less objective than the scientist's attempt to integrate all available data about physical phenomena into a theory. As in textual interpretation, the more integrative and elegant the scientific formula, the more convincing it is, but, as every scientist knows, hardly any theory about complex natural phenomena is ever final.

How texts expand our world

Hermeneutic thinkers believe that the goal of textual interpretation is to expand our vision of the world. As we learned in Chapter 3, by 'world', they mean the totality of meaningful relations that we share through common signs and symbols. In face to face conversations, we communicate our perceptions about something directly employing mimicry and gestures. We are much like a tour-guide who can point to things and thus describe a world of interconnected meanings. Literary, philosophical, and historical texts, however, are detached from this immediate situational context. Texts, as we already pointed out, are cut off from living speech and thus must relate meaning differently.

In the humanities, we encounter works containing cultural, social, and intellectual ideals, important subjects that tell us something about how the ancient Greeks, for example, or 19th-century Victorians viewed their world. As Paul Ricoeur explained, such texts speak of possible worlds and of possible ways of orienting oneself in those worlds. In contrast to Romantic hermeneutics, we no longer seek an author's meaning behind a text, looking to commune with another soul, or fusing two minds through words. According to Ricoeur, the emphasis is no longer on a reader trying to transfer himself into the spiritual life of another person. Nor does interpretation seek to isolate the meaning intended by the original author at the moment of writing. We neither try to understand the other's innermost experience nor to establish a single self-identical meaning, but rather to enter the world that the text displays and to explore the possibilities this world opens up for us. For example, when we read Plato's *Republic*, what vision of human nature and society are revealed to us? When immersed in Edward Gibbon's *The History of the Decline and Fall of the Roman Empire*, what do we learn about Rome's vision of life and Gibbon's interpretation of it? An interpreter thus aims at authorial intention only insofar as she seeks to grasp the propositions about a world the author communicated by means of the text.

Readers are thus confronted by an object they cannot simply bend to their personal preferences. Rather, interpretation of texts (as we have seen) follows the movement Gadamer called the 'fusion of horizons'. The reader confronts the world projected by the text. The social and moral world suggested by Tolstoy's novel *Anna Karenina*, for example, suggests a certain vision of life. While this vision is culturally determined by the author's own time and concerns, it nonetheless engages us on perennial human issues, such as social responsibility, faithfulness in marriage, and the nature of religion. A reader's understanding of himself in his world is confronted by the text's world. When asking 'what is my view of marriage?' or concluding 'I never thought about religion in this way', the reader's own horizon is expanded, his self-understanding challenged and changed. According to hermeneutic philosophy, the hermeneutic circle of understanding is thus not a movement between two subjects, the author and the reader, but rather between my understanding myself in my own world on the one hand, and the world projected by the text with its possibilities for life, on the other.

Literature and the importance of metaphor

Within the humanities, hermeneutic thinkers have paid particular attention to literary texts, because they demonstrate more intensely the power of language to turn our environment into a meaningful human world through symbolic representation. Literary texts reveal two important aspects of how our imagination works. The first is that language is not primarily conceptual but metaphorical. Word pictures or metaphors are not mere frills, but essential to perceiving a human world. We describe nature around us through language that relates everything to human concerns. Just think of how often you have heard the term 'mother nature', by which we evoke an inherent order and purpose. Another example of how we humanize the environment is through spatial metaphors. We are so used to thinking of things as 'up' and 'down' that we forget how deeply spatial metaphors determine our understanding of the world. For example, if we want to be realistic instead of religious, philosophical, or artistic, we prefer to descend, to 'get down' to the facts, or 'get down' to business. We also associate edifying thoughts or religious experience with 'lifting us up'. The point is that humanizing the environment, the kind of thing that poetry does, is more natural to us than defining things in abstract conceptual language. Many hermeneutic thinkers insist that poetic language is more native to us than scientific language. They refer in this context to the essential 'metaphoricity of language' that structures our thought.

Second, literary texts, and especially poetic works, demonstrate that understanding itself functions the way metaphors work by integrating two apparently different things in a way that enlarges our perspective. When the poet Robert Burns declaimed that love is like a red, red rose, and that he would love his 'lass' while 'the sands o'life shall run', he juxtaposed a human emotion with natural objects, resulting in a deeper understanding of love. This act of integration is precisely the kind of mediating performance Gadamer posited as the essential interpretive movement of human understanding: we integrate something unfamiliar into our familiar way of seeing things. In doing so, our own former perspective is altered by being enlarged and deepened. Hermeneutic philosophers consistently emphasize the power of the human imagination to envision and inhabit a meaningful world through language. At the heart of imagination lies metaphor, our ability to see similarity in difference and thus to enlarge our perspective and see things otherwise. Scientists also rely on this imaginative power of integration for scientific discovery. In both the sciences and the humanities, only a well-trained imagination can see things otherwise, think outside the box, and come up with new social visions or scientific paradigms.

Defending the humanities

Given the importance hermeneutic philosophers attribute to metaphor, language, and the imagination, it should come as no surprise that they ardently defend the humanities as central to society. Hans-Georg Gadamer, for example, explicitly framed his main work, *Truth and Method*, as a defence of the truth conveyed by art as necessary for human life. For all the hermeneutic thinkers presented in this volume, interpreting texts in the humanities educates our imagination through immersion in our cultural inheritance, thereby allowing us better to appreciate the present and envision the future. Indeed, it seems indisputable that the well-being of society depends on cohesive social visions and also on our ability to imagine things differently. The inability to do so usually leads to simplistic entrenchment in received truths and to a fearful defence of what has always been. In short, lack of imagination often results in fundamentalism.

Natural science, economics, and politics depend on literature, philosophy, and religion for educating the imagination. Every chapter in this book shows that we cannot oppose facts to values, but that all facts are integrated into meaningful wholes through a personal commitment to some kind of vision of how things ought to be. If this universal hermeneutic claim is true, then the shaping of our imagination through historical, philosophical, and literary texts in the humanities is indeed paramount.

Hermeneutics and the digital humanities

A recent trend in the humanities with hermeneutic implications is the emergent field of digital humanities. This movement began in the late 1960s with the application of computational methods to the traditional work of preserving and analysing texts. Just as quickly as computers developed, however, computing in the humanities went from mere storing and encoding of texts for keyword searches to the digitization of libraries and the emergence of complex search models for comparative analysis of texts. Researchers today can cross-reference literary texts with other social information from letters, birth registries, or wills and testaments in a matter of minutes. Without question, this digital revolution has radically improved the availability of cultural resources. For example, obtaining rare books or works in different languages even decades ago required extensive travel or expensive postage, whereas any interested party can today access such resources on a laptop.

While appreciating this ease of access, scholars in the humanities are also asking the important hermeneutic question of how this digital revolution changes the conditions for understanding texts. At least some digital humanities scholars are well aware that computational methods are not neutral but predetermine an interpretive grid. This begins at a base level with representing texts digitally through encoding them in certain formats, and extends to constructing concordances that allow us to search texts according to key words. Who decides which words or metaphors are more important? Already, such encodings are an interpretation. Whether search parameters for digital models of analysis are set for similar word recognition, or for meaning content, each parameter represents the text through a particular, pre-selected focus. Still, digital humanities advocates hope that complex combinations of digital representations of texts can increase our understanding of them. Critics, however, warn that computation follows a mathematical model of reasoning that is good at listing information but bad at making creative inferences from literary works. Computing, in other words, is not a substitute for understanding.

Thus from a hermeneutic standpoint, the crucial question is whether one should concede the basic assumption made by many digital humanities proponents that this essentially mechanical computational model is in any significant way analogous to human understanding. No doubt, computational representations of texts and their cross referencing with related sources from, let's say, sociology or archaeology, provide a greater breadth of information than hitherto thinkable in the humanities. As has been demonstrated in Chapter 3, however, interpretation depends on the personal integration of information into a meaningful whole. Such integration requires an imagination that is educated and centered in a cultural tradition.

For example, analysing Plato with the help of computational models, however complex, is not a substitute for spending time with Plato, reading his texts, understanding his argumentation, his way of seeing things. We recall from previous chapters how much interpretation depends on the tacit background knowledge we carry with us. It is not our detachment from, but familiar relation with, an interpretive framework that allows us to grasp the meaning of something. To return to our reading of Plato and computing, only by having lived with the works of Plato, by indwelling them and thus feeling at home in them the way we feel at home in our house or city, will we be able to use digital technology responsibly. Such familiarity allows us to evaluate patterns discovered by a search engine rather than becoming dependent on them. While digital technologies are powerful, we have a tendency to transfer from our imaginations to our digital tools the responsibility of coming up with new insights. Tools, however, are merely as powerful or useful as the skill and imagination of the person employing them.

Chapter 5
Hermeneutics and theology

Theology, as the German theologian Karl Barth once said, is a human word about God's word. Theology, in other words, interprets divine revelation. This is especially the case for the three major monotheistic or Abrahamic religions (Judaism, Christianity, and Islam), the so-called 'religions of the book'. For these faiths, religious identity and daily living depend on divine revelation as collected in a sacred text. The Jewish Torah, the Christian Bible, and the Quran are believed to be divine revelations, and therefore have binding authority and define communal life. In all three religions exists a natural kinship between divine and human law, since believers hold that God reveals laws for righteous living, some of which became part of modern civic law. Together with jurisprudence, theology is thus one of the classic hermeneutic disciplines that demonstrate the intrinsic practical dimension of interpretation: how does the law or God's revealed will apply to our present concerns? Neither the legal nor the theological interpreter is satisfied with a mere historical, descriptive understanding of the text. Only in application does the text do its work as law or proclamation.

Hermeneutics and divine inspiration

A central hermeneutic issue in theology is the relation of divine revelation to human understanding. All three Abrahamic religions believe in a divinely inspired text. Does a divinely inspired text require interpretation? Interpretation, we have argued, entails the faithful translation of what someone has said about a certain matter into our own meaning context. The interpreter is essentially a mediator who relates the meaning of another's communication to present circumstances. Understanding what someone says to me cannot be merely the ability to repeat word for word a sentence or a text. Rather, when I have understood something, I can put its meaning into my own words.

Divine inspiration, however, seems contrary to hermeneutics. Does not inspiration ensure the absolute clarity of God's revelation by avoiding any human mediation? If indeed God dictates every word to a prophet or apostle, then we have the one place that is exempt from interpretation. If divine inspiration is indeed dictation, the original human recipient merely channels God's truth without any understanding. Such divine dictation, however, also affects how later readers approach the text. Belief in inspiration without mediation through human understanding encourages fundamentalism. If a sacred text itself is deemed perfect and unalterable, believers are prone to disregard the historical context of prophecies, or pay no attention to literary genres. The result is that only a strictly literalist reading counts as the straightforward and faithful access to revelation. Most importantly, if interpretation inescapably filters a text through the reader's own cultural horizon, fundamentalists' disregard for their own historical context will virtually ensure that they read their own predilections into the text. Consider, for example, the fundamentalist reading of the creation story in Genesis as literalist scientific account rather than as mythological narrative about the human condition. What, however does inspiration entail in the three religions?

Inspiration and Judaism

Ancient Jewish prophets were 'filled by God's Spirit', when speaking for God, and traditionalists hold that the first five books of the Hebrew Bible, the *Torah* (or what English scholars call the *Pentateuch*, Greek for 'five books'), were dictated word for word by God to Moses, while the remaining sacred writings were more generally inspired. In a broader sense, *Torah* can also refer to the entire biblical narrative or even the totality of Jewish teaching, culture, and practice. At the same time, this view of verbal inspiration did not blind interpreters to historical inaccuracies in the text, but these were regarded as challenges to the human understanding rather than evidence against the trustworthiness of divine revelation.

Nor did respect for divine inspiration automatically require literal reading. Biblical scholars often read passages allegorically when they seemed to contradict human reason. Jewish hermeneutics thus always contained elements that allowed for the broadening of conceptions of inspiration from strict verbal dictation to the more general notion that emerged with reform movements in Judaism during the 19th century. This modern view of inspiration still accords the biblical text special divine status, but also recognizes the human mediation of God's revelation by acknowledging different authorial styles, composition of single texts from multiple source materials, internal contradictions, and anachronisms in the Bible.

Inspiration and Islam

This transition to a more hermeneutic view of inspiration has been more difficult for Islam due to its unique view of the Quran as verbally inspired, divine incarnation. Similar to traditional Rabbinical views of the Pentateuch's inspiration, the vast majority of Muslims hold that the Quran 'is the speech of God, dictated without human editing'. According to Islamic tradition, captured in this medieval illustration, an Angel dictated the pre-existing Quran word for word to the prophet, who memorized Allah's revelation by recitation (the root meaning of the word 'Quran' is to recite). Flames depicting contact with the divine were also used in Judaism and Christianity to indicate visions or revelations of the divine. The prophet's reception of a written text from the Archangel, however, emphasize this idea of verbal inspiration (see Figure 5).

For most Muslims, the Quran is 'the eternal, uncreated, literal word of God (*kalam Allah*) sent down from heaven, revealed one final time to the Prophet Muhammad as a guide for humankind'. As 'uncreated', the Quran is divine, an extension of God himself. Muslims often liken the Quran to Jesus as God's incarnation. Just as Jesus is God's eternal word made flesh, so the Quran embodies 'the eternal divine word'. In common with its sister religions, Islam had to wrestle with the relation of reason to divine revelation, but, as scholars have pointed out, the notion of an eternal text raises particular hermeneutical issues. For example, while Christians hold the gospels to be accounts written by inspired authors as witnesses to Jesus as God's self-revelation, the Quranic text in its specific form *is* God's word. For Muslims, the Quran *as* Quran exists only in its original Arabic transcription. Any translation of it is no longer the Quran but 'an interpretation of its meaning'.

Scholars of religion have drawn attention to another hermeneutic consequence of the Quran's theological status. An eternal text implicitly 'negates the very idea of it having a historical context'. How can one reconcile the notion of an uncreated text with the fundamental hermeneutic insight that all truth is mediated historically? How do principles of historical textual criticism widely accepted by modern scholarship apply to the Quran? This question pits traditionalists who lean towards ahistorical, literalist readings of the Quran against modern Islamic reformers such as Tariq Ramadan, who emphasize '*ijtihād*', the hermeneutic application of original Quranic statements to later historical contexts.

Indeed, Muslim scholars throughout the centuries, have operated on the assumption that while the text is infallible, its interpreters are not. Most main schools of Islamic interpretation have rejected

5. A medieval depiction of the prophet Muhammad receiving the revelations of the Quran from the Archangel Gabriel.

simplistic literalist readings of the text, and scholars have long debated allegorical interpretation and the role of reason in understanding divine revelation. The most famous Muslim attempt to reconcile Quranic inspiration with human reason was made by the great medieval Muslim philosopher Ibn Rushd (Averroës; 1126–98) who argued for two levels of truth. 'The divine law', he believed, 'is divided into two parts, the external sense and the interpretation.' Common folk should read literally, adhering to the external sense as expressed in pictures and allegories, lest they fall into unbelief. Unlike 'the multitude', interpretation is reserved for 'the learned', philosophers whose erudition enables them to see the unity between divine and human reason. Averroës' elitism may be irritating to modern ears, but his effort to unite faith and reason remains an important hermeneutical issue in theology.

Inspiration and Christianity

Like its sister religions, Christianity features various views of inspiration, ranging from a general sense of divine illumination that includes human mediation to a narrow doctrine of dictation. This narrow doctrine is called 'verbal inspiration', the claim that God showed the human author exactly what words to use. The concept of verbal inspiration emerged relatively late in Christian history after the Protestant Reformation. Verbal inspiration became necessary to establish a stand-alone, self-interpreting Bible, by which an individual reader could attain certain truth divorced from tradition and ecclesial authority.

Originally, however, Christian interpreters worked with a broader sense of inspiration. New Testament writers refer to the scriptures as 'God-breathed' (2 Timothy 3:16), and Christianity generally understood this term to mean that human authors act as scribes who mediate God's word through writing in their own cultural idiom, as depicted in Caravaggio's classic portrayal of St Matthew's inspiration (see Figure 6). Note that the picture shows

6. The Inspiration of St Matthew (1602) by Caravaggio.

no sign of direct transmission such as a beam of light; on the contrary, the angel speaks from a dark background, and the saint listens carefully as he notes down the received revelation.

This motif of mediation becomes even more emphasized through the central Christian doctrine of the incarnation, the teaching that God revealed himself most clearly through the actions and words of Jesus. The New Testament *Letter to the Hebrews* includes a classic expression of this view: 'In many and various ways God spoke of old to our fathers by the prophets; but in these last days he has spoken to us by a Son, whom he appointed the heir of all things, through whom also he created the world. He reflects the glory of God and bears the very stamp of his nature, upholding the universe by his word of power' (Hebrews 1:1–3). The Christian doctrine of the incarnation teaches that God entered history and time by becoming a human being, and thus also becoming subject to interpretation. John's gospel offers Jesus's self-designation as interpreting God: 'no one has ever seen God; the only son who is in the bosom of the father *interpreted* him' (John 1:18). The Greek word for 'interpreted' is '*exēgēsato*', the word from which we get our English word exegesis, another term for interpretation. Thus central to Christian hermeneutics is the idea that Jesus is the 'exegete' of God, who interprets him through his own life.

In principle, the idea of the incarnation as the final self-revelation of God establishes interpretation at the very centre of the Christian faith. According to Christian belief, in Christ the eternal word of God expresses itself through human words and thus becomes subject to interpretation. As a modern Catholic theologian, Hans-Urs von Balthasar (1905–88), put it, Jesus is the perfect interpretation of God whom we have to interpret in turn. We only know God through the incarnate Christ and Christ only through our interpretations of him, which themselves are always in the 'flesh' of history. The incarnational pattern of God's self-revelation presents the Christian with the double hermeneutic challenge that Hans-Georg Gadamer, as previously mentioned, labelled the 'fusion of horizons'. Not only does the Christian interpreter have to reconstruct God's own self-interpretation *within* 1st-century Middle Eastern culture and history, but he also has to translate what the text says into his own life context determined by modern preconceptions and concerns. Awareness of both contexts is necessary for a faithful interpretation.

The importance of tradition

Hermeneutic philosophy insists on the importance of tradition for understanding. Hans-Georg Gadamer, as noted, emphasized tradition as the medium that shapes our consciousness and thus connects us to the past. The interpretation of religious texts puts historical flesh on this hermeneutic claim. Even adherents of verbal inspiration will have to admit the indispensable role of community and tradition for interpretation. As we shall see, the Quran itself, though held to be unmediated dictation, still requires interpretation through tradition. Similarly, the framework of meaning within which the collection of biblical writings is read is based on the religious community's beliefs and expectations about God's relation with them. This framework itself is based on the history of interpretation within this community and its collective religious experience as it developed over time. In short, what the Bible means is inseparable from the interpreters, who over time and as members of a community canonized the texts and contributed to their definite contours of meaning. Just as the Hebrew Bible is only what it is based on tradition, so the Christian Bible is read *as* Bible only within the tradition of the church. This, of course, is precisely Gadamer's point about historically effected consciousness and tradition being positive forces for understanding.

Tradition and the Hebrew Bible

Many scholars agree that what we hold in our hands today as the Hebrew Bible is the result of a dynamic process of recording and interpreting narratives by scribes who collected oral or written accounts, compiled them, and wove them into coherent narratives; this dynamic process, called *redaction*, means that interpretation played an intrinsic role in the very origin of the Bible. This process was intensified in 587 BCE, when Israel was conquered by the Babylonian empire, the temple at Jerusalem destroyed, and the majority of Israelites deported to Babylon. Without the temple, the Torah, consisting of the essential historical narratives and laws together with their interpretations mostly by teachers called 'rabbis', became central to the identity and life of the Jewish community. Even after the restoration of Jerusalem and the temple, following Israel's return half a century later, the lasting shock of the Babylonian captivity was likely responsible for the increasing codification of the Hebrew Bible or *Tanakh* (completed between 3rd and 2nd century BCE) and of the long tradition of rabbinic oral commentary on the Bible, called the Talmud. Most biblical scholars agree that during this post-exilic period, the biblical narrative was consciously reshaped to answer Israel's gnawing questions in light of the exile: 'why did this happen to us?' and 'are we still the chosen people of God?'

A typical example of redactive re-interpretations of biblical texts within an ongoing tradition occurs in the book of Chronicles. In an earlier narrative, the prophet Nathan assured King David that his dynasty would last: '*your* house and *your* kingdom shall be made sure forever before me' (2 Sam. 7:16). Post-exilic writers staring at the rather meager replacement of Solomon's (David's son's) temple knew for a fact that Nathan's prediction had not come about. The redactor of Chronicles solves that problem by shifting the emphasis from David's house to God's house: 'I will confirm him in *my* house and in *my* kingdom forever, and his throne will be established forever' (1 Chron. 7–14). God, in other words, has not forsaken Israel, because David's kingdom was merely a symbol for what God would ultimately accomplish through the Davidic line; God will put his man on the throne in good time and vindicate Israel. The old text thereby gains a new and forward-looking aspect.

Such internal reinterpretations of the Hebrew Bible did not mean that scribes simply invented new narratives, but that they engaged in the fundamental hermeneutic activity of interpreting existing texts in light of their own cultural horizon, especially since they believed themselves to be part of God's ongoing story with Israel. Through this interpretive collating and handing down of texts, a certain set of sacred writings became the defining core of Israel's identity as God's people. These texts merged into the biblical 'canon', the Greek word for a plumb-line or measure. For Jewish interpreters, the texts within this collection shed light on each other and they cross-reference topically related texts, reading passages within the context of the entire Bible to understand God's will for the believer.

When interpreting the Hebrew Bible, Jewish scholars also draw on the Bible's history of interpretation. The three main sources for this tradition are the Mishnah (rabbinic commentary on the Torah delineating legal application for social mores), the Talmud (scholarly commentaries on the Mishnah), and Midrash (rabbinic explanation of biblical texts concerning legal application and spiritual meaning). Drawing on these sources, a Jewish scholar never reads individualistically but always in conversation with the interpretive tradition.

Tradition and Christian interpretation

Tradition also plays a central role in the Christian religion, not least because Christianity is a conscious re-interpretation of Israel's biblical narrative. Christianity began as a Jewish messianic movement grounded in the same biblical narrative that presents Israel as symbolic of humanity's fall and ultimate redemption by God. Early Christian theologians continued the Judaic tradition of reading the Hebrew Bible as an evolving story of God's dealings with Israel, and identified Jesus as the Messiah who realized the story's climax. The apostle Paul expresses this sense of continuity with Israel's narrative when he interprets the Christian message as 'promised beforehand through [God's] prophets in the holy scriptures, the gospel concerning his Son, who was descended from David according to the flesh, and designated Son of God in power according to the Spirit of holiness by his resurrection from the dead, Jesus Christ our Lord' (Romans 1:1–4). We have to keep in mind that Paul develops his theology before the Christian Bible with its division into Old and New Testament existed. The 'holy scriptures' that provide the imagery and interpretive categories for Paul and early Christian theology is the Hebrew Bible.

The gospel narratives of Matthew, Mark, Luke, and John follow the apostle Paul's lead by interpreting Jesus's life and work with reference to these scriptures. Indeed, they present Jesus himself as framing his own actions in light of the scriptures' narrative. According to John, Jesus tells people 'If you believed Moses, you would believe me, for he wrote about me' (5:46). Following Jesus's own claim to be Israel's promised Messiah (in Greek the *Christos* or 'anointed one'), early Christians fundamentally changed the Jewish interpretive framework. As the promised Messiah, Jesus had fulfilled God's ancient promise of a new covenant, according to which God would be immediately present among his people, his very word written in their hearts. Therefore, his disciples' writings about him become known as the new covenant, or 'New Testament', and the Hebrew Bible became the 'Old Testament'. The writings that eventually formed the New Testament were canonized through use and circulation among Christian assemblies, with a recognizable core set of writings extant (including epistles by the apostle Paul and the four gospels) as early as the late 2nd century. Both in the Hebrew and Christian traditions, formal canonization of biblical writings recognized a core set of texts already established as central by communal practice.

Clearly, tradition is as important for Christian interpretation as it was in Judaism. Both religions read their scriptures in light of an ongoing tradition that provides the hermeneutic framework or whole within which texts are read. For Christian interpreters,

Christ and his redemptive work for humanity constitute the hermeneutic whole to which each interpretation ultimately points. From the beginning, this theological key determined the interpretive relation of Old and New Testaments. As the church father Augustine expressed it in the 4th century, the New Testament is *latent* (contained in seed) in the Old and the Old, *patent* (its meaning made obvious) in the New.

Early theologians employed two hermeneutic principles to read the Bible in light of the life and teachings of Christ. The first is called *typology* and was meant to show how important events in Israel's narrative anticipated the Christian faith. The word *typos* meant 'imprint' or 'pattern', and indicated an Old Testament event or person pointing to a future reality. The apostle Paul saw in Adam a 'type' whose original purpose of life with God was fulfilled in Christ (Rom. 5:14). Similarly, other events in the history of Israel are *typoi* or examples that reveal God's will for the Christian church.

The second interpretive principle was *allegorical* reading (from *allos*, other and *agoreuein*, to speak). Allegorical interpretation showed how a historical event or biblical statement becomes a symbol pointing to another meaning. For example, Paul interpreted the story about Abraham's two wives allegorically, thereby revealing the Christian reinterpretation of Judaism, whereby not Torah but Jesus provides access to communion with God (*Galatians* 4:21–7). In Paul's reading, Hagar a slave represents the 'old' Mosaic covenant and Sarah, a freewoman, points towards the new covenant of promise as fulfilled in Christ.

Spiritual interpretation

Ancient Christian interpreters practised typological and allegorical readings to uncover the spiritual meaning of biblical texts in order to deepen their understanding of God. They did not consider such readings fanciful or arbitrary because they had a different view of reality from us moderns (see Chapter 2). Ancient interpreters assumed a connection between mind and a higher order of reality. For them, sacred texts were windows to divine realities. Theologians call this the 'sacramental' quality of language and texts, that is, their ability to mediate transcendent, divine truths. Already in the Greek philosophical use of Homer or in rabbinic interpretation of the Bible, the text was not read in a strictly literal or historical sense. In contrast to modern literalism, texts were treated as cryptic, containing hidden spiritual insights. Even historical events were means of conveying spiritual truths.

Christians continued this tradition in their own way: if indeed Christ was the incarnation of God's creative wisdom and power, and if indeed his life was the climactic fulfilment of the biblical narrative, then the spiritual meaning of biblical histories, prophecies and proverbs must ultimately refer to him. For this reason, early Christian readers had no problem adopting interpretive strategies common to the ancient world, such as typological and allegorical readings, in trying to unveil the deeper, spiritual meaning of the text. For example, when God told Moses to remove his sandals before the burning bush, Gregory of Nyssa (335–94) found in this event the moral principle that just as Moses removed his leather sandals to approach God, we must put off immoral behaviour when interpreting the Bible. Gregory believed that we cannot comprehend the light of divine truth unless the 'dead and earthly covering of skins' is removed from the 'feet of our soul'.

Medieval interpretation continued with the same basic theological hermeneutic. The text's ability to serve as window to spiritual realities was eventually captured in a well-known motto memorized by theology students: *Littera gesta docet, quid credas allegoria, moralis quid agas, quo tendas anagogia* (the letter teaches what happened; what you are to believe the allegory; the moral sense what you ought to do, and the anagogy where you're tending, i.e., a passage's eschatological meaning). This formula

Hermeneutics and theology

was not a rigid method for squeezing every ounce of spiritual truth out of the biblical record, but simply acknowledged the possibility that a text could have more than one meaning. One of the greatest medieval theologians, Thomas Aquinas, showed us how this interpretive strategy worked for God's command, 'Let there be light', in the first chapter of Genesis: 'For when I say, "Let there be light", referring literally to corporeal light, it is the literal sense. But if it be taken to mean "Let Christ be born in the Church", it pertains to the allegorical sense. But if one says, "Let there be light", in other words, "Let us be conducted to glory through Christ", it pertains to the anagogical sense. Finally, if it is said "Let there be light", in other words, "Let us be illumined in mind and inflamed in heart through Christ", it pertains to the moral sense.'

The rule of faith

The Christian reading of the Bible is not immediately evident from the text itself but requires the guidance of tradition. To be sure, early Christian theologians did not think they imposed an interpretive grid on the text but were convinced that close reading justified their theological insights. Yet they also recognized that the biblical text itself does not automatically provide their theological perspective. The recognition and elaboration of the Christian hermeneutic circle thus depends on tradition, that is, on the interpretive patterns laid down by Jesus and his first followers. The apostle Paul, well trained in rabbinic exegesis, knew that the interpretation of the Bible required guidance from tradition. For this reason, he emphasized, along with other New Testament authors, the handing down of the tradition (the Greek word is *paradosis*) about Jesus.

As the icon to the right shows (see Figure 7), the set of ancient Christian interpreters after the New Testament writers, known as 'the church fathers' for their formative role in the development of theology, recognized the importance of tradition for understanding the Bible. The icon is dedicated to the importance of intercessory prayer, picturing the enthroned Christ, flanked by Mary and John

7. Icon depicting the importance of scripture and interpretive tradition.

the Baptist, who intercede in prayer along with other apostles and saints. The hermeneutical importance of this icon, however, lies in the centrality of the scriptures for the life of faith. Note that, in the middle of the image, Christ holds a book. Christ himself, whose life and work open up the meaning of the scriptures, points to the scriptures as the medium that illumines his mission and his teachings. Christ as the word made flesh and the written word thus form an inseparable hermeneutical circle of whole and part that illumine each other.

The apostles and disciples, who also hold and study books, are depicted in the icon as interpreting the Bible in light of Christ's teaching, with the church as the communal centre for lives formed by reading and prayer. The church fathers referred to this interpretive tradition as 'the rule of faith', or, in the words of the 2nd-century church father, Irenaeus, as 'the canon of truth'. This canon of truth was a basic summary of Christian doctrine, handed down from the apostles, emphasizing Christ as the unifying 'mind of the scriptures' and stressing the redemptive work of Jesus as incarnation of God on behalf of human beings.

Tradition in Islam

In contrast to the Jewish and Christian Bibles, which attained their final form through a gradual interpretive process, the Quran is presented as an unedited, complete divine transmission, dictated to Muhammad by the Archangel Gabriel. Much scholarly debate surrounds the assemblage of these revelations that were gathered into the first standardized version of the Quran about twenty years after Muhammad's death (632 CE). Even the claim of the Quran's uncreated perfection, however, cannot circumvent the essential role of tradition for interpretation. Far from being self-explanatory, the Quran's own form as a collection of dictated revelations requires an interpretive framework from outside the text itself. Islam scholars have pointed out that unlike the Hebrew or the Christian Bibles, the Quran does not offer 'a continuous narrative' structure that provides a narrative framework for interpretation. Instead, this larger whole within which Muslims interpret God's particular revelations to Muhammad is provided by the history of interpretation, which begins with recorded events about the Prophet's own implementation of Islam during his lifetime. The *Hadiths* are first-hand reports about the Prophet's sayings and actions, collected over a period of centuries, first passed down orally and later collected as written texts.

Muslims recognized that Hadiths possess varying degrees of reliability. They have, for example, designated two Hadith collections the *sahihain* or 'two sound ones', as possessing the highest authority to define Islam next to the Quran. Religion scholars have observed that the Hadiths contain a lot more material on legal and practical norms for the Muslim faith than does the Quran. This normative legacy is called the *Sunna*, and provides the framework of practical reasoning for interpreting the Quran. Hence the Quran will not be the best place to go for the curious reader who inquires about a particular issue in Islam. Islam scholars explain that the Quran 'is not a book of law, and main tenets of Islamic theology are never mentioned in the holy book'. Advice on dress codes, marriage laws, and the nature of jihad or education for women is not found in the Quran but in the Sunna.

Traditionally, Islamic legal scholars, the Imams or Muftis, are the interpretive authorities to whom an ordinary Muslim turns for legal advice concerning practical Muslim law or *Sharia*. In making his interpretive announcement, the legal scholar who has spent his life studying the Quran along with its interpretive tradition, draws on the Quran, on applicable Hadiths, and on preceding judgements by other scholars from various schools of interpretation. Islamic legal experts thus demonstrate the dependence of Islam on interpretation through tradition. Even while the Quran itself is regarded as direct revelation unmediated through history or human culture, understanding this sacred text requires its mediation through tradition. In short, just as in Judaism and Christianity, hermeneutics is central to the Islamic way of life.

In recent history, the importance of tradition for Islamic interpretation has been challenged by more individualistic interpretations of the Quran from two groups. The first group are radical Islamists, who circumvent interpretive tradition by reading the Quran selectively to support their own political ends. The second group is a peaceful Reform movement within Islam somewhat analogous to the modern Protestant attempt in Christianity to understand the Bible based on individual reason alone. Referring to themselves as 'Quranists', reformers examine the Quran on its own terms, explicitly rejecting the authority of Hadith and Sunna. A recent reformist translation of the Quran (2007) appeals to those 'who prefer reason over blind faith', and 'who seek peace and ultimate freedom by submitting themselves to the Truth alone'. Again, just as Protestant Reformers sought to liberate the Bible from its hermeneutic confinement by church authority, Islamic reformers want to free the interpretation of the Quran from the clergy's authority and past traditions, entrusting 'salvation only to God's signs in nature and scripture'. They hope that freeing the Quran from tradition will unite believers and demonstrate the text's moral imperative of justice for every human being.

A game changer: the Protestant Reformation

In Western culture, the development of hermeneutics was closely connected to the interpretation of the Bible. The Protestant Reformation of the 16th century was a defining event in the history of hermeneutics because it brought about important hermeneutical changes. While Reformers continued the theological tradition of reading the Bible with reference to Christ, conscious reliance on tradition was eventually lost, as the slogan 'the Bible alone!' (*sola scriptura* in Latin) gradually divorced biblical exegesis from the interpretive tradition of the church. The Reformation thus prepared the way for the historical-critical study of the Bible and the modern view that the Bible is to be read like any other text.

The German priest Martin Luther (1483–1546), a central figure of the Protestant Reformation, asserted the Bible's interpretive independence and clarity. The Bible, he wrote, 'is through itself certain, easily accessed, and comprehensible, its own interpreter (*sui ipsius interpres*) that tests, judges and illumines everything'. Luther's view of the scripture's perspicuity eventually developed into views of the Bible for which Luther would have had very little sympathy, such as, for example, theories of verbal inspiration, or (at the other extreme) the kind of historical criticism that examines the Bible as historical source document or a literary artefact without reference to the church.

Luther's insistence on *sola scriptura* may have helped separate theology from exegesis, but his own exegetical practice demonstrates that he never envisioned a Bible separate and independent from the church. Our picture of Luther translating the Bible illustrates his reliance on tradition. Note that he is surrounded by books, which symbolizes his dependence on other interpreters (see Figure 8). Luther instinctively recognized that the Bible is always read through *some* interpretive lens, because he wrote numerous prefaces to the Bible as a whole, and to individual books, to offer 'those who are not familiar with it, instruction and guidance for reading [the Bible] profitably'.

Aside from providing interpretive guidelines for the reader, Luther constantly interacted with various church fathers in his exegesis, and also frequently asserted doctrines such as infant baptism and even the immaculate conception of Mary (born without sin) on the strength of church tradition and in the absence of convincing exegetical evidence. In short, even while asserting a self-interpreting Bible, Luther's biblical hermeneutic flowed from a deeper theological framework that provided a dogmatic orientation or 'rule of faith' for guiding biblical exegesis. The same may be said of the Reformation tradition in general.

The rise of modern historical criticism

Nonetheless, Reformation rhetoric had put a wedge between tradition and biblical interpretation, a separation that was further

8. Martin Luther, translating the Bible into German while hiding in the Wartburg. Original illustration from 'Martin Luther' by Gustav Freytag (1847).

encouraged as biblical interpretation increasingly became the professional activity of academics who were only loosely connected to religious communities. Through these developments, the Bible was transformed from a sacred book of the church into a foundational classic text of Western culture. This dislocation of biblical studies from the church into research universities illustrates powerfully the influence of social changes and institutions on interpretive habits.

The divorce of biblical interpretation from the life of the church was accompanied by the changing view of truth discussed in Chapter 2. Now the meaning of religious texts had to match the intellectual horizon of interpreters disengaged from history and tradition. Objective truth was now defined by the disengaged mind of rationalist philosophy. According to the historical critic Samuel Reimarus (1694–1768), Christian revelation must be 'free from contradiction', and show the same evidential clarity as mathematic equations.

Biblical content was true, in other words, when it corresponded to modern epistemology. For example, miracles don't happen today; thus, biblical miracles were descriptions of natural occurrences by primitive minds unschooled in modern science. Moreover, if people didn't rise from the dead, and the walls of Jericho did not crumble at the blast of trumpets, how trustworthy was the biblical narrative as a whole? Armed with this suspicion, historical criticism departed radically from ancient interpretive practices by looking *behind* traditional interpretation to the *real* historical events and *real* people, making up the *real* Bible that lies obscured under the layers of traditional interpretation. 'Objectively real', in this case, meant whatever conformed to the historian's preferred rationalist construal of what may or may not have happened.

Today, influenced by hermeneutic philosophy, a large number of biblical scholars question the rationalist assumptions of historical criticism. They especially distrust its modernist view of history, according to which the disengaged self examines historical facts as scientific objects 'out there', completely separate from the historian's own evaluation of them. For hermeneutic theory, this division between neutral historical facts and their subsequent evaluation is impossible because the historian selects facts based on some tacit belief about their relevance.

No doubt, biblical interpretation has benefited immensely from historical criticism. Archaeological finds, source criticism (discerning the socio-historical origin and compilation process of texts) and form criticism (determining literary conventions of form and meaning) have greatly enriched modern understanding of biblical material. At the same time, however, and all too often, the supposed objective historical interpretation read its own modern predilections into the text in the name of objective scholarship. Many historians and biblical interpreters today agree with the hermeneutic insight that the historical reconstruction of the past is never neutral, but depends necessarily on the web of significance within which the historian locates the facts.

If all interpretation thus depends on prior beliefs about reality, the historical critic's superior authority collapses together with his appeal to a purely scientific reading of the text. Theological readings of biblical texts can no longer be dismissed out of hand. Moreover, scholars now also realize that the rationalist premise of historical criticism can readily fall prey to the same literalism that characterizes fundamentalist readings. Unlike pre-modern belief in a multi-layered meaning of words and texts, Rationalism and Fundamentalism share the same non-hermeneutic view of truth, fuelled by their obsession for the one true interpretation.

Beyond historical criticism: Barth, Bultmann, and Bonhoeffer

Early in the 20th century, Karl Barth (1886–1968) called for a return to theological interpretation. In his famous commentary on the book of Romans (1918), Barth attacked historical criticism's philosophical assumptions and championed reading the Bible once again as God's direct address to humanity. Barth insisted that academic historical criticism had recast the Bible in the image of accepted modern categories of meaning. This narrow interpretive grid prevented the text from conveying its divine message in freedom and with authority. Another important theological figure to wrestle with the question of how a modern mind can understand an ancient sacred text was the German Lutheran theologian Rudolf Bultmann (1884–1976).

Bultmann complained that Barth merely asserted the Bible as God's word, but failed to address the hermeneutic problem of mediating between ancient and modern worldviews. Ancients had believed in spirits, demons, miracles, and the cosmology of a pre-scientific age; moderns believed in empirical science and technology. Bultmann asked, what does the New Testament mean for us today quite independently of its mythological setting? Theology, he argued, must undertake the hermeneutic task of stripping biblical truth 'from its mythical framework, essentially "demythologizing" it'.

Yet Bultmann's own interpretation relied heavily on the existential philosophy of Martin Heidegger, and ended up reducing the gospel to an inner transformation marked by authentic living in freedom, by a 'self-commitment in faith and love'. The Lutheran theologian and Nazi-resister Dietrich Bonhoeffer (1906–45) agreed with Bultmann that Barth's theology avoided the hermeneutic mediation of past and present. Bonhoeffer disagreed, however, with Bultmann's reduction of the gospel to an 'inner self-commitment', because it obscured the Bible's comprehensive vision of this present world as belonging to God.

This vision required not mere inner piety but included political responsibility, and therefore denied what one particular group of Protestants calling themselves 'German Christians', then firmly believed, namely that one could be a good Christian and a good Nazi at the same time. Bonhoeffer who stood for the opposing 'confessing Church', recognized that how Christians interpret the Bible matters greatly for their understanding of political responsibility and their willingness to resist political tyranny.

Some recent hermeneutic trends

In the 20th century, hermeneutic philosophy has increasingly influenced Christian theology in particular. The British theologian Anthony Thiselton (1937–), for example, did much to introduce English speaking scholars to the philosophical hermeneutics described in Chapters 2 and 3. Phenomenology and hermeneutics also played a large role in Catholic thought, and Eastern Orthodox scholars such as Andrew Louth (1944–) have drawn extensively on Gadamer's hermeneutics to argue for a return to theological interpretation. Theological interpretation treats the Bible as the book of the church and therefore as more than a historical or literary document. A theological hermeneutics 'concerns the role of Scripture in the faith and formation of persons and church communities'.

In recent decades, greater awareness of interpretive presuppositions has led to three major hermeneutic models that respect the integrity of biblical texts and are more conducive to theological hermeneutics. The first is 'narrative theology', pioneered by the Yale theologian Hans Frei (1922–88). Inspired by Karl Barth, Frei wanted the text to speak with its own theological voice. This hermeneutic respects the plain and narrative presentations of the biblical texts as coherent wholes, and establishes their 'literal sense' with reference to the biblical narrative, before worrying about any other application to the present. For these reasons, Frei rejected Gadamer's insistence on applicatory reading (see Chapter 2), and believed we must first objectively establish the plain meaning of the text before evaluating its significance for us.

Historical criticism itself is also undergoing a shift away from a purely scientific to a more literary approach. The Old Testament scholar John Barton (1948–), for example, retooled traditional historical criticism by arguing against the caricature of historical critics as scientists, who dissect the text dispassionately. Rather, biblical scholars are simply literary critics who, without any theological commitment to view the Bible as God's word, appreciate its literary quality and narrative unity. This updated historical criticism still dismisses, however, the hermeneutic claim that understanding a text entails its translation into the present by fusing past and present horizons. Rather, 'meaning before application' is the motto of the critical exegete, who understands first what the text meant and then applies that meaning to modern issues.

A third, more hermeneutic approach is canonical criticism advanced by Yale Old Testament scholar Brevard Childs (1923–2007). Fully aware that no object of investigation is simply 'given', canonical criticism consciously adopts the historically developed, received biblical canon and the apostolic rule of faith as the hermeneutic whole that determines the meaning of individual texts. Canonical criticism affirms the hermeneutic claim that neither authorial intent, nor a text's meaning for an original audience, is normative. Rather it looks to the communal intent that guided canon formation. Not unlike pre-modern readers, canonical interpreters take a broad view of divine inspiration. They reject the fundamentalist belief that every single word of the text is divinely inspired, and rather speak of general divine guidance in canon formation, allowing for the characteristic marks and frailties of human authorship. Aside from Canonical Criticism, interest in theological readings of the Bible in the context of the church has markedly increased among Catholic and Evangelical scholars in Britain and North America.

Chapter 6
Hermeneutics and law

What has hermeneutics to do with the law? Everything—even though this may not be obvious at first glance. Many constitutions in Western democracies begin by defining legislative powers. Article one, section one of the American constitution, for example, determines that 'all legislative Powers herein granted shall be vested in a Congress of the United States, which shall consist of a Senate and House of Representatives'. The American and other constitutional documents frequently mention 'the rule of law' or 'the due process of the law', as the nation's fundamental way of regulating all social relations. (This book is written for an English-speaking audience and therefore the content of this chapter refers almost exclusively to the common law tradition.)

Such formulations reinforce the popular opinion that the law is unambiguously given and simply needs to be enforced. Many lawyers and laypeople share the conviction that the work of legal experts and judges is simply the mechanical application of existing legal propositions to specific cases. The fact that much legal work boils down to devising contracts or adjudicating violations of civic law also strengthens the idea that legal interpretation is the disinterested application of rules. The more unbiased and impersonal this application, the more impartial and just the judgment. Justice, after all, has been traditionally depicted as a blindfolded goddess, *Iustitia*, who, after weighing the evidence in the scales with complete impartiality, wields punitive power, symbolized by the sword. This portrayal of legal practice does not appear compatible with our argument that interpretation is intrinsic to all human knowing.

Legal work, however, is always more than mechanical application of legal propositions to specific cases. Indeed, any practical legal argument, whether consciously or not, is based on jurisprudence, that is, on a theory about the nature of law. Iconography provides us with a clue that, contrary to popular belief, law depends on more than rules. Changing images of justice indicate changing theories about the meaning of law. Note, for example, the changes from the ancient Roman image of justice depicted in Figure 9 to its later Christianized version in Figure 10. In Greco-Roman culture, human law was grounded in a higher universal moral order. This universal 'natural law' formed the basis of human civic law, and was ascertainable by reason. Human laws were, in a sense, rational interpretations of a more diffuse, greater moral framework. Violation of this moral order, represented by the Greek goddess Themis or the Roman equivalent Justitia (see Figure 9), would be weighed impartially (symbolized by scales and blindfold) and punished (sword).

With the Christianization of the Roman legal tradition, the nature of law changed. Reason was now only a partial and highly unreliable guide to law. Instead, God's moral law as revealed in the Bible became the ground of civic law in Christendom. Note that in the right picture, the goddess now holds a book instead of the scales (see Figure 10). This book reflects the view of Christian law theorists, such as Samuel Pufendorf (1632–94), that natural law itself is ultimately derived from the Old Testament God, who had revealed it most clearly in the Ten Commandments, which formulated the optimal moral code for human flourishing. The corrupt, selfish nature of human beings, however, required the enforcement of law through penalties. The New Testament gospel, by contrast, was thought to provide the ultimate motivation for

9. Lady Justice (Justitia), blindfolded.

10. Lady Justice (Justitia) with the Bible.

obedience to this code, since it was no longer based on fear of punishment but on love of God and neighbour. This development in the history of law shows us that legal practice depends on underlying assumptions about the grounds and nature of the law. Contrary to the popular understanding of law as static application of rules, legal practice is hermeneutical all the way down. To judge is to interpret.

Legal positivism: the law is the law

It is a widespread assumption, shared by many lawyers and a number of legal philosophers, that 'the law is the law'. On this view, the law is a set of legal propositions that lawyers and judges apply to certain cases by means of a shared set of rules. The American legal philosopher Ronald Dworkin (1931–2013) called this ideal 'the plain fact view' of the law, and neatly summarized its working assumptions:

> The law is only a matter of what legal institutions, like legislatures and city councils and courts, have decided in the past. If some body of that sort has decided that workmen can recover compensation for injuries by fellow workmen, then that is the law. So questions of law can always be answered by looking in the books where the records of institutional decisions are kept [...]. Law exists as plain fact, in other words, and what the law is in no way depends on what it should be.

The appeal of the 'plain fact' ideal is similar to the attractiveness of the scientific method: while one needs special training to do science, anyone using the right tools and procedures can potentially do science. Likewise, legal training is necessary to find precedents and understand the arcane vocabulary in which they are recorded, but the facts are simply given, lying ready at hand for those who know how and where to look for them. For the plain fact view adherent, interpretation can only mean the clarification of a legal proposition's logic and obvious sense. On this view, interpretation in the hermeneutic sense of mediating past and present, motivated by personal interest, implies relativism.

The plain fact view of the law is a form of legal positivism, which derives its name from the Latin word *positum*, that which is set down or posited. Legal positivism is less concerned with the theoretical grounds or ideal meanings of laws than with their factual historical existence. The influential English jurist John Austin (1790–1859) made this distinction to argue that legal theory should focus on the law as posited: 'The existence of law is one thing; its merit and demerit another. Whether it be or be not is one enquiry; whether it be or be not conformable to an assumed standard, is a different enquiry'. Austin was not opposed to the then still popular notion that all human laws ought ideally to conform to divine laws, but he did deny that jurisprudence should concern itself with this relationship. Jurisprudence ought to deal with the positive law of a land as it stands, rather than indulge in philosophical speculation about what the law ought to be. According to Austin, a judge simply executes the letter of the law without consideration of its relation to eternal justice or some other moral measure outside existing law. Should a judge dislike a positive law, he should have the legislative power to make a new one, but he should not pretend that he is interpreting a positive law as it *ought* to be understood in accordance with a broader or higher moral norm.

Hart and the hermeneutics of recognition

For Austin, positive laws were legislated by a sovereign power such as a king or a group of legislators to whom subjects have to render obedience. A century after Austin, the legal philosopher Herbert L. A. Hart (1907–92) replaced Austin's concept of positive law as sovereign command with a more democratic ideal. In modern law-based societies, the authority of law depends on people's acceptance of a law's enduring validity. For example, a speed limit of sixty miles per hour in a certain state remains valid not simply because a sovereign lawgiver imposed it on those who have no choice but to obey. Rather, in a society ruled by law such restriction remains in force because people elected a body of representatives who imposed them, and because people have accepted, and continue to accept, the legitimacy of the government and police to uphold this law.

Rules of recognition

The whole point of legal positivism is to come up with a standard for distinguishing valid from spurious legal judgments. What in a modern legal society is the test for valid law? Hart's answer is 'rules of recognition'. For him, two sets of legal rules operate in society. We have primary rules that tell us not to steal or not to kill, and how property should be bought or sold, and so on. We also have secondary rules 'of recognition', by which primary positive law is recognized and applied in a regulated manner. Such rules provide the kind of legal stability that sets modern law-based societies apart from more traditional communities governed by social conventions that are less reliable and can easily change.

For example, let's say in a pre-modern agricultural community, there are varying rules by which land can be bought and sold. We can imagine the ensuing uncertainties and quarrels in land transactions. A stabilizing rule of recognition would be that a publically recognized court, following certain procedures, can make legally valid pronouncements on land claims. For Hart, this recognition of courts and procedures is the ultimate test of law's validity. This 'master rule of recognition' allows stable juridical practice on the basis of interlocking rules that recognize legal precedents and that allow for controlled change of laws. In complex societies, such as the United States for example, these rules acknowledge a written constitution, entrust its enactment to a legislature, and recognize legal precedents. We also acknowledge a certain hierarchy of rules that ranks written legal statues over custom and common law precedents.

For Hart, law was all about rules. Legal work is not unlike a science experiment. Just as a scientific fact is validated by a general rule under which it fits, a legal pronouncement is validated by the rules of recognition, that is, by adhering to established legal practice. Indeed, Hart likened a judge to an umpire who makes the final call (judgment) based on the sport's acknowledged rules. Hart insisted that legal practice is validated by accepted social conventions for a law's validity and use. Particularly court officials and those involved in legal procedures adhere to 'unstated rules of recognition'. Hart correctly observed that judges inhabit these rules, and often use them the way Heidegger described the use of hammer, as something we employ without assuming a theoretical or external stance toward the tool.

Other legal philosophers have criticized Hart's attempt to establish the validity of law on verification through rules. American philosopher of law Dennis Patterson (1948–), for example, denied that deciding legal cases is like a science experiment. He argued against Hart that historical precedent often provides no clear guidance, and that rules of recognition do not guarantee a decision's validity. Rather, deciding a case requires legal arguments based on existing law. By contrast, legal positivists

> like to think that even if the rules by which a judge arrives at a final sentencing cannot be demonstrated with scientific exactness, a ruling can still be shown to be impartially derived from generally-accepted rational principles and legal rules.

New laws or the limits of legal positivism

Can we really verify the application of law by rules? Legal positivists think so, but other legal theorists argue that interpreting law requires consideration of moral argument that goes beyond mere application of rules. And indeed, quite often, existing rules are clearly insufficient to resolve a case. In the civil law case *Riggs v. Palmer* (1889), for example, a New York court had to decide whether an heir named in the will of his grandfather could inherit under that will, even though he had murdered his grandfather to obtain the inheritance. The court admitted that under the existing legal rules, the property would have to go to the murderer. In fact, one judge suggested a simple application of the existing rules: the murder was to be punished according to the rule of law but no rule existed to add to this punishment the withholding of the inheritance.

Obviously, this strictly rule-based judgment went against the moral sensibility of the majority, who thus also appealed to the principle that 'all laws as well as all contracts may be controlled in the operation and effect by the general, fundamental maxims of the common law'. The court then cited the maxim of equity: 'no one shall be permitted to profit by his own fraud or to take advantage of his own wrong, or to found any claim upon his own iniquity, or to acquire property by his own crime'. In this case, the court used its discretionary legal power to move from mere application of existing rules to legislate a new rule that prevented the grandson from receiving the property. Legal positivists would argue that this case was an exception that went beyond the normal application of rules and required the judge to make a new law. The judge acted as *legislator* by establishing a new rule based on a moral principle external to the legal system, in this case the maxim of equity.

An updated form of legal positivism, called 'legal conventionalism', would arrive at the same conclusion. Like legal positivism, conventionalism argues that legal practice does not depend on political or moral reasoning, but rests on prior legal decisions that are in turn based on established, tried and true legal conventions. America's legal convention, for example, makes law through statutes enacted by congress or the state legislatures in the way prescribed by the Constitution. A court working with this legal tradition arrives at a ruling based on the conventions established by prior legal history and practice. Should these conventions be insufficient to arrive at a ruling that makes sense, the court has the discretion to go beyond established conventions and make a new law. For legal positivists, 'new laws' are exceptions that prove the rule that law is all about rules. From a hermeneutic point of view, however, such examples show that law requires more interpretation than positivists are willing to admit.

Critics of legal positivism

Legal positivism depends on three main assumptions. First, law should be seen primarily as a social fact without necessary reference to moral considerations. Second, laws and legal decisions are valid insofar as they make sense according to a coherent, rational application of texts and rules that are ensured by a particular society's institutionalized 'rules of recognition'. Third, thus what is a right and a duty is explicable within such a system, and only in exceptional circumstances requires consultation of external universal moral rights or duties. Other legal movements have challenged this plain fact view of the law as a self-regulating system of rules.

Legal realism

One such school, which flourished from the late 19th century well into the 1960s, is 'legal realism'. Legal realists contest the positivists' 'plain fact' view of the law, and stress the personal, political, and economic influences in legal practice. They argue that the collective experience reflected in the common law, together with judges' political and personal views of social welfare, necessarily determine legal decisions. In light of the great law-making (legislative) power exercised by judges in many countries, cynical legal realists sometimes conclude that legal decisions depend on what the judge had for breakfast. Legal realists, however, help us recognize the interpretive role of personal or political influences in law making, and they rightly focus on the actual, realistic outcome of legal decisions that must go beyond adherence to the letter of the law. Legal realists are sceptical about idealistic views of the law, whether as an objective, rule-based system, or as grounded in a universal ethics.

Natural law

Natural law is another theory highly critical of legal positivism. In contrast to both legal realists and legal positivists, natural law adherents insist that positive human law is accountable to a more universal moral law. They hold that the interpretation of law always involves a normative, moral dimension. Natural law theorists fear that by denying this intrinsic connection between law and morality, positivists and realists could encourage the validation of law based on efficiency alone. The claim that valid legal decisions derive their authority from rules within the system can also have bad practical consequences.

The Austrian legal theorist Hans Kelsen (1881–1973), for example, advanced a 'pure theory of law', according to which the validity of legal procedures is measured purely by their legitimacy within a legal system, whatever their ethical import may be. Natural law adherents fear the consequences of such thinking. If valid law is primarily defined by its function within an efficient legal system based on social custom, and if obedience is justified by a rationality intrinsic to this system, how does this protect against obedience to inhuman laws? What argument would legal positivism have against characters such as the Nazi Adolf Eichmann, who defended his mass-murder of Jews by saying that he simply did his duty as legislated by the law of the Third Reich? The positivist Kelsen, who had to flee Germany on account of his Jewish ancestry upheld the formal validity of law even in the Nazi state. For this reason, natural law theory has traditionally asserted universal human rights, such as human dignity, freedom, and equality. Such rights precede and ground any legal system, and thus help us resist the kind of systemic tyranny suggested by our Eichmann example.

Legal positivists in turn, are not very fond of natural law, mostly because they reject as outmoded the view that the cosmos itself exhibits intelligible order, and that nature thus contains discernibly right and wrong ways of doing things. For legal positivism, no such universal reality exists. Thus, natural law is either rejected altogether or reduced in metaphysical content to such things as the universal human desire to survive and the consequent need for legal restraints that ensure such survival. Moreover, legal positivists fear that natural law undermines positive law. Positivists separate empirical law from a higher moral order to highlight the positive role of cultural traditions and prevent a creeping anarchy: to say that a law's validity and true justice depend on some ultimate universal standard of justice sounds great; yet history exhibits many different versions of universal morality. Combine this plurality with individual choice, and we'll soon have individuals deciding for themselves which laws they should obey. For natural law theorists, of course, this appeal to universal morality is essential to avoid legal tyranny, even if such tyranny were sanctioned by democracy.

Hermeneutic conceptions of law: to judge is to interpret

The 'plain fact view' of the law appeals to many because it makes legal work look like a science in which results are obtained and verified through rule-governed analysis. On this view, disagreements between judges and lawyers must be traceable to practical mistakes in rule application or an unwarranted intrusion of politics and social activism into law. Such intrusion is said to occur when judges interpret the law to say what they think it ought to say rather than what it *actually* means. Judges are then perceived to 'innovate' or to twist the law to fit their agenda rather than simply to apply the law as it stands.

According to hermeneutic theory, however, the plain fact view misrepresents how legal practice actually works. The ideal of knowledge that validates results through impartial observation and rule-governed analysis is taken from the natural sciences and misapplied to jurisprudence. By contrast, legal theorists who embrace a hermeneutic conception of law argue that jurisprudence is much more like the kind of interpretation we practise when reading literature. To be sure, such interpretation relies on certain interpretive rules for establishing a legal text's meaning and historical context. Yet how a judge brings these rules to bear on a case is ultimately guided by her underlying assumptions about the law's moral purpose and function within a given society. As in the *Riggs v. Palmer* case, the ruling required amending rules of precedent with the help of a general maxim ('no one shall be permitted to benefit by his own fraud etc.'). This ethical guideline derived not from rules of law but from the general moral consensus that a murderer should not receive his inheritance even if the legal system permits it.

In short, a legal judgment involves more than the mere application of rules. Legal ruling is an act of interpretation in which a judge establishes the meaning of legal texts by 'translating' them from their particular historical context into the present. But this is not simply rule based. Rather, this translation is exactly the kind of creative performance Gadamer had called participation in an 'event of tradition'. In making his ruling, a judge intuitively draws on many assumptions that do their work quietly in the background, such as the language, legal concepts, and moral expectations of his tradition. In poring over legal texts, the judge's interpretation is directed entirely by the goal to understand what a particular legal statute means for the present case. Thus, legal practice is a prime example of Gadamer's claim that reading texts with any degree of understanding always includes application. It is only in the light of the present case that the judge knows what a legal statute really means. Interpreting a legal text and studying a poem in English class thus follow the same basic hermeneutic movement. The stakes, of course, are different.

Textualism

One example of a consciously hermeneutic approach to law is
textualism. As the name suggests, textualism focuses on the
interpretation of legal texts, such as statutes and constitutions.
Textualists recognize that law cannot be reduced to a system of
logical rules. They argue that the interpretation of legal texts has
become paramount because most important legal norms and rules
that determine our lives come from federal bodies, such as the US
congress, and other legislatures; for example, in America, every
issue of law resolved by a federal judge involves the interpretation
of a society's written regulations, statutes, or constitution. Textualists
worry that in the absence of clear hermeneutic guidelines, judges
will use their great authority to interpret legal texts in light of
political interests, and thus engage in 'judicial law making' (see
Figure 11). And if judges get to make laws rather than elected
representatives in legislatures, then the courts' interpretation of
the law begins to undermine democracy.

Textualists are not literalists. They know that the meaning of a
legal text is not simply 'obvious' but needs to be construed by the
reader. The prominent American textualist judge Antonin Scalia
(1936–) proposed the following interpretive guideline: 'A text
should not be construed strictly, and it should not be construed
leniently; it should be construed reasonably, to contain all that it
fairly means'. But according to what criteria do we establish the
intended meaning? We can now see that textualists clearly
confront the hermeneutic issue of authorial intent we already
encountered in Ricoeur's discussion of literary texts.

How should we define 'intent'? Like Ricoeur, textualists refuse to
define intent as an author's inner state of mind at the point of
writing, from which an interpreter determines what a writer
wanted to say. Chasing after authorial intent is a futile undertaking
because we will never figure out what the author or lawgiver *meant*

"Call it 'legislating from the bench,' if you will, but on this occasion I should like to repeal the First Amendment."

11. Legislating from the bench.

to say. Indeed, the case of law is even more complex because we are now trying to figure out what each legislative member may have wanted to express. Legal historians can scour every record of debates on the floor during a law-making process and not arrive at any consensus on what each member may have wanted the law to say, let alone get at the collective intended meaning defined in this way.

To avoid the wild goose chase of authorial intent, textualists follow Gadamer and Ricoeur in focusing not on what the author *intended* to say but on what he actually *said* in the text. Textualists don't care what the intention of a legislature was in drafting a law but what the written words mean. Textualists' criterion for the proper meaning of a legal text is how those who ratified it would have understood its meaning in the original social context. For this reason, textualism is also known as *originalism*. Textualist interpreters ask what a document such as the US constitution would have meant to a citizen in the 18th century with a reasonable command of the English language.

A good example for textualist hermeneutics is the question of whether the death penalty is constitutional. For textualists, it is clear from the historical context and from a common sense reading of the constitutional text that the founding fathers endorsed capital punishment. Why else would, for instance, the Due Process Clause of the Fifth and Fourteenth Amendments say that 'no person shall be *deprived of life* without due process of law'? And yet many judges claim the death penalty to be unconstitutional based on the Eighth Amendment's denying the federal government the right to impose 'cruel and unusual punishments'. Textualists complain that these judges read modern moral attitudes into the text and then rationalize this practice by talking about a 'living constitution' that evolves with changing times. This evolution may be required, but textualists worry about the motives for such change. They worry that an 'evolving constitution' will cease to be a guidepost but become a mere mirror of rapidly changing social mores and a plaything of political interest. It is no wonder, they argue, that appointments of judges have become a hot political issue, because the courts have become the main instrument for constitutional change. In the words of judge Scalia, 'If the courts are free to write the Constitution anew, they will, by God, write it the way the majority wants […] By trying to make the Constitution do everything that needs doing from age to age, we shall have caused it to do nothing at all'.

Law as integrity

The constitutional expert, Ronald Dworkin, understood the textualists' worry of interpretive relativism, but criticized their own lack of a hermeneutic principle that could explain how a judge applies the original meaning of a legal text to present cases. Textualists speak about following the general thrust or trajectory of the original text, but such a process requires itself some kind of higher principle. If, for example, the founding fathers' endorsement of the death penalty is clear from the constitutional text, how does following its general trajectory help if current American society seems to agree that such a penalty violates human dignity? What kind of hermeneutic principle allows us to translate the meaning of the constitutional text into our present circumstances without turning the Constitution into a mere tool of present public opinion or politics?

Dworkin suggested the ideal of 'integrity' as a regulative principle for legal interpretation. In common usage, 'integrity' is synonymous with 'honesty', but Dworkin's usage points to a deeper meaning of the word 'integrity'. We call people honest, because their lives form a coherent whole in light of which their particular actions make sense. He argued that in the same way, judges should make their decisions by considering individual legal statutes and rulings within the history of our legal tradition as a whole. According to Dworkin, American legal history and society support a certain moral principle of human dignity and equality by which we all implicitly measure fairness and justice.

Dworkin located the source of this principle in the French revolution's idea of the common brother and sisterhood of all human beings, but he did not pursue the religious roots of this concept. He simply accepted it as the prevailing moral framework of American society. Judges who accept this ideal will not simply be guided by rules (legal positivism), nor fall prey to the political whims of the moment (judicial activism) in making their decisions. Instead, they treat legal cases in the same way that a historian narrates history, a theologian reads a sacred text, or a literary scholar interprets a play, poem, or novel. The judge considers the entire interpretive history of preceding rulings that bear on a given case to see what emerges as the essential content of relevance for the present case. At the same time, the judge applies this content in light of the generally accepted principle of integrity—in our case, the principle of equality.

For example, in the case of the death penalty, a judge could argue that capital punishment should be deemed unconstitutional because the founding fathers' endorsement conflicts with the idea of human dignity which they also held and to which we still appeal for equality; we can thus detect a kind of hermeneutic circle between a particular legal statute, such as the constitution, and what the constitution is generally about, namely the fair and just administration of American society based on a certain ideal of what it means to be human. The ideal of human dignity functions as a greater principle of integrity, as the whole, by which every individual ruling can be assessed. This helps prevent law from becoming a system of directionless rules that can be turned into tools of state oppression; at the same time, the emphasis on the history of interpretation and legal precedents bearing on the case acts as interpretive restraint that prevents courts from hijacking the constitution for the latest popular fad. Free for creative application that is constrained by interpretive tradition and also guided by moral principles beyond the law, legal practice shows itself to be deeply hermeneutical without succumbing to relativism. To judge is to interpret.

Chapter 7
Hermeneutics and science

Facts or interpretation?

The word science, from the Latin *scientia*, simply means
'knowledge', and thus describes every area of human knowing.
Especially in the English language, however, science is associated
with the natural or exact sciences, such as physics, biology,
chemistry, and mathematics, in contrast to the humanities. It
seems natural for us to distinguish between these two areas
of human knowledge in terms of verifiability. Science seems
to offer us the simple and certain facts of reality, while artistic,
religious, and philosophical views about life are mere interpretations
of the world. Science, we have learned in school, rests on strictly
empirical observation, on accurate measurement, and on the
exact verification of its results. In contrast to religion, art, and
literature, scientific knowledge is independent of received
opinion, personal bias, and the vagaries of language. In short,
it would appear that all the elements we have outlined as
intrinsic to hermeneutics do not apply to science. Scientists
know facts, while philosophers, artists, and theologians peddle
matters of personal taste. Scientists know; everyone else
merely believes. This view of science, while no longer shared
by most scientists, originated in the 18th and 19th centuries,
and remains stubbornly lodged in our collective popular
consciousness.

Scientific objectivism

'Scientific objectivism' is the view that science's empirical method leads to the highest form of knowledge, namely objective truth as defined by scientific experimentation. There are, of course, good reasons for the origin of this view. Medieval natural philosophy had been strong on reason and logic, but conducted virtually no scientific experiments. Alchemy, the late medieval precursor to chemistry, did much to encourage experimental science, but also remained wedded to a metaphysical, and even magical, view of the world. Modern science, by contrast, earned its enormous reputation through medical and technological breakthroughs based on predicting the material causes and effects of natural phenomena.

Take medicine, for example: today we no longer treat fever by bloodletting to balance the body's 'humours', but we take aspirin or acetaminophen because scientists managed to isolate the chemical process in our body that causes inflammation. Scientists at the forefront of this scientific revolution blamed the unscientific approach of their medieval and Renaissance predecessors for the slow advancement of research and technology. The British scientist Sir Francis Bacon (1561–1626), for example, complained that medieval scientists had started from certain axioms dictated by theology or natural philosophy, and then tried to figure out how empirical facts fit this framework. For instance, they endlessly discussed the possible existence of a vacuum by comparing Aristotle metaphysis with Christian notions about the nature of the universe. Instead of trying to interpret the world from philosophical texts, however, they should have conducted practical experiments. The typical researcher of his day, Bacon lamented, 'flies from the senses and particulars to the most general axioms', which he does not question but takes to be settled. True science, however, should be based on practical experimentation and proceed inductively. It should start 'from the senses and particulars, rising by a gradual and unbroken ascent, so that it arrives at the most general axioms last of all'.

Bacon's inductive method, moving from particular facts to general principles, was characteristic of a new era in science that emphasized experimentation and verifiable results. In time, however, this corrective emphasis on induction became its own settled axiom that, ironically, obscured the way scientific knowledge actually works. The role of a framework for integrating facts, the personal involvement of the researcher in the process of scientific discovery, her imagination, passionate commitment, and faith in being on the right path to discovery—all these essential aspects of science were overlooked. In part, this distortion was due to the growing belief, arising in the 18th century, that the universe is a gigantic machine, governed by physical laws discoverable through impartial observation. For such a mechanistic conception of the world, science is purely descriptive. Knowledge is what happens to the detached observer, whose personality, disposition, and imagination contribute nothing to scientific discoveries. This systematic elimination of the knower from the process of knowing with a sole focus on the object of knowledge is called 'scientific objectivism'.

Scientific positivism

The French astronomer and mathematician Pierre-Simon Laplace (1749–1827) articulated a highly influential form of scientific objectivism called 'positivism'. Positivism claims to rely exclusively on established scientific facts for explaining the world. Laplace loved the idea that scientific facts would eventually reveal all general physical laws by which the world functioned, and thus render the world predictable. His dream was that 'all the forces by which nature is animated and the respective positions of the entities which compose it, [...] would embrace in the same formula the movements of the largest bodies of the universe and those of the lightest atom: nothing would be uncertain for it, and the future, like the past, would be present to its eyes'.

Scientific knowledge is thus modelled on a mechanic's understanding of a machine: know the parts and how they function in relation to each other, and you know how the whole mechanism works. To explain how a mechanism works, therefore, is also to understand it, but understanding no longer involves any personal relation to the knower, but concerns simply a functional grasp of a mechanism or instrument. Knowledge, in short, is simply a mass of information and therefore strictly objective insofar as it is devoid of any value or meaning. Factual knowledge comes *before* we form opinions about the meaning or purpose of such information. We can now see that a certain theory of science initiated the basic split between fact and value we have already observed earlier in Hirsch's interpretive theory and in legal positivism.

Laplace thus formulated the ideal of strictly objective knowledge that became deeply lodged in Western culture and still holds sway in many quarters: science has nothing to do with meaning but is all about observational accuracy, precision, and predictability. For this very reason, Laplace's ideal of science is really a delusion that equates information about particular facts with the meaning these facts have for us. This creates the illusion that human experience is reducible to the knowledge of the material conditions for such experience. Even in our day, this remains the temptation of reductive materialism, the idea that love is nothing but chemistry, and that morality finally comes down to genetic fine tuning.

Along with others, the French philosopher and sociologist August Comte (1798–1857) extended Laplace's mechanistic ideal of knowledge to our understanding of society as a whole. Comte added a historical dimension to scientific objectivism, by claiming that human knowledge in every field has to run through three developmental stages. The first is the theological or fictional stage in which theories about the world are dominated by the religious and poetic imagination. The second metaphysical or abstract stage is the disillusionment with the first stage, when gods are replaced by philosophical systems to explain human experience, and when old social orders are erased through revolutions. This negative movement is then followed by the third positive stage, when the now mature human spirit reforms society based on a factual understanding of the world.

Comte understood that facts only make sense within some kind of a theory, but in contrast to the theological and metaphysical stages, the positivist method will aim to generate its theories increasingly from established facts alone, and thus put education and social reformation on the secure empirical footing of the laws of nature. The true positive method, wrote Comte, 'consists above all in seeing in order to foresee, in studying what is in order to conclude what shall be, according to the general dogma of the invariability of the natural laws'.

Thinkers like Comte are largely responsible for spreading scientific positivism (or objectivism) to non-scientific fields of knowledge, such as sociology and political theory. Researchers in the humanities were tempted by positivism's lure of verifiable knowledge and sought to convert their disciplines into exact sciences. The school of analytic philosophy, for example, started when philosophers such as Rudolf Carnap (1891–1970) and Bertrand Russell (1872–1970) sought to verify truth statements by means of a logical rules. Today, scientific positivism, with its dream of scientific predictability, has long been discredited as illusory by many philosophers and modern scientists. The essential flaw of trying to shore up truth based on impersonal methods of verification is that judgements and insights require personal commitments—trust in a theory or belief in the basic rationality of the universe—that are not themselves subject to verification by rules. Put differently, there is no rule for how we apply rules.

Nonetheless, positivism's desire for certainty is hard to eradicate from the popular imagination. Are we really immune to the tempting thought that human progress consists in controlling human nature and regulating social trends? Have we really outgrown the idea that true knowledge is guaranteed by scientific methods of verification?

Understanding as a basic mode of intelligent life

Scientific positivists were wrong to buy objectivity at the cost of eliminating the personal, subjective elements that characterize every human endeavour to know. As in any other area of human knowledge, science too is very much a matter of interpretation. As we have shown for other knowledge disciplines (philosophy, theology, and law), to acknowledge that all human knowing requires interpretation does not promote relativism, but actually helps us to affirm objective knowledge in a way that goes beyond the old divide between subjective belief and objective knowledge.

The philosopher of science Michael Polanyi (1871–1976) argued that understanding, defined as the integration of particular details into a meaningful whole, is a basic mode of learning common to all intelligent life. Polanyi showed that understanding is not a theoretical concept, but originates in the most basic impulse inherent in living species from the lowest animal to our own kind, namely to control and master one's environment.

Any attempt to make sense of one's situation, whether practically or mentally, is indeed an act of understanding. When, for example, a laboratory rat is taught to navigate a labyrinth and the setup is changed, she will first try to negotiate the novel arrangement based on the internalized understanding of the original, first maze. Trial and error eventually result in a new understanding, and each new adjustment will occur more quickly. Similarly, in experiments with chimpanzees, scientists have observed the same basic elements of mental activity exhibited by humans in seeking solutions to problems. Apes faced with the problem of obtaining food placed well out of reach outside their cage, for example, first recognized the problem, ruminated about it, came up with a stratagem, and then sought to verify their idea by putting it into practice. They also showed elation when obtaining their goal.

Contrary to the 19th-century ideal of the scientist as independent, detached observer, who accumulates facts until a general pattern or law of nature emerges, we have to realize that scientific research and discovery follow the intensely engaged interpretive pattern we have just described. Scientific research and discovery do not require detachment, but are based on personal involvement focused on a better understanding of reality.

Personal knowledge

Scientific knowledge shares with every form of human knowing involved commitment, whether we co-ordinate our eye muscles to focus on a distant object, or bring to bear our education and cultural background on the meaning of a text. In both cases, we are integrating a number of subsidiary elements to focus our task. Gadamer called this focal awareness the 'applicatory' dimension of hermeneutics. Polanyi called it the *from–to* pattern of knowledge. We think *from* and through our received knowledge and prior experiences *towards* our goal, bringing this know-how to bear on a certain task. In pursuing this goal, we do not, in fact we cannot, stop to verify our received knowledge. To do so would disrupt its subsidiary instrumental function.

Think, for example, about the various subtle counterbalancing movements required to ride a bike. Were we to focus on these instead of our goal of moving ahead, we'd surely fall down. In the same way, a scientist straining to understand something inhabits and uses scientific axioms without constantly doubting or verifying their truthfulness while he is working on a problem. Polanyi called this subsidiary element 'the tacit dimension' of knowledge. The scientist too participates in these structures, and wields them in striving for a new understanding of a phenomenon, the same way we wield a hammer to drive in a nail. We are aware of the handle and its vibrations in our hand, and we keep adjusting our aim and blows to focus on hitting the nail. Should we divert our attention from the nail to the hammer itself, we'd most likely merely hit our fingers.

Polanyi's concept of tacit knowing makes essentially the same point as Heidegger's 'in-order-to' structure of knowing: trying to understand the world around requires an engaged rather than a detached self. Gadamer made the same point by emphasizing the role of tradition as the tacit background that we inhabit and that guides our perception. All human knowledge, including science, follows this skilful pattern of inhabiting an activity whereby we integrate our intellectual movements and passions to focus on a goal. Indeed, even empirical observation (as demonstrated by the muscle coordination needed to focus the eyes) rests ultimately on the integration of such subsidiary elements to a focal centre. Knowledge is thus always the action of integrating particulars into a coherent whole. And this integration does not happen all by itself but requires personal engagement. As in any area of human knowledge, this integrative work depends on the training, personal convictions, and imaginative power of the scientist. Scientific knowledge, as much as artistic knowledge, depends on this personal dimension for success.

Science as art

The no-nonsense, take-it-or-leave it reputation of science rests on the belief that science delivers simply facts, allowing for the exact prediction of results based on impersonal computation. Adherents to this still popular image of science, however, overlook a crucial personal element on which the natural sciences depend: the scientists interpret facts based on experience in order to make predictions. This personal element becomes clear when we compare scientists' interpretation of data to reading a map.

A map represents a part of the earth's surface in a similar way to how experimental science represents our experience of reality. Now, we all know that we cannot read a map simply by reading a book about map-reading, or by memorizing rules about map reading. Rather, reading a map depends on our personal judgement and our skill as map readers. We first have to link our actual position in the landscape with a point on the map, then on the map we must find the way towards our destination, and, finally, we have to identify this path with the help of physical landmarks.

And just as the correspondence between the map and the actual landscape depends on our judgement, itself based on personal skill and experience, so any exact science requires a trained eye and personal judgement for correlating instrumental readings or mathematical computations with the reality of actual experience. The reading of gauges and dials, as well as the compensating for marginal deviations of calculations are interpreted by scientists within the context of their respective field and their intuitive understanding based on years of training. Thus scientific observation, just like map reading, is not an exact impersonal numbers game, but requires the personal judgement of the scientist. Scientific prediction depends on an art, namely the art of establishing—by means of the scientist's trained eye, ear, and touch—the correspondence between the explicit predictions of science and the actual experience of our senses to which these predictions apply.

Another telling example for the need of personal experience and judgement in scientific knowledge is a doctor's use of anatomy in making a diagnosis. A medical student, who has freshly memorized all the anatomic schemas of the human body from her science textbook together with descriptions of every illness, is not therefore automatically equipped to diagnose illnesses. Even extensive training on dead bodies in the pathology laboratory is no substitute for the experience acquired by a doctor or surgeon that allows him to see the body as a living, functional unit. Good knowledge of anatomy is of course necessary and immensely helpful, but, as with the reading of maps, integrating this information within the context of the living body as known from decades of practice sets apart the experienced medical practitioner or surgeon. Thus, insofar as scientific knowledge requires the artful integration of details into a coherent whole through an act of the imagination based on personal experience, science too relies on interpretation.

The hermeneutics of scientific discovery

Philosophers of science have long questioned the ideal of science as an impersonal and strictly rule-governed process. Norwood Russell Hanson (1924–67) and Paul Fyerabend (1924–94), for example, affirmed that scientific observation is not unbiased but always 'theory-laden'. Scientific theories are like lenses through which the researcher interprets findings. They thus confirm for science the contextual quality of observation Heidegger had called 'seeing-as'. Still, in the popular imagination, scientific discovery happens gradually, simply through controlled experimentation. According to this portrayal of scientific progress, carefully building on previous findings, the scientist would never affirm anything that has not been tested and verified by experience, and would drop a theory the moment an observation turns up which conflicts with it. In reality, however, scientific discovery is much more dynamic and much less predictable.

First, science relies on tradition insofar as scientists hold to a certain vision of reality or world picture as currently accepted by science. No one scientist actually knows and, least of all, constantly verifies every detail of this reality. Moreover, scientists are inducted into the world of science and its experimental methods as an apprentice learns from a master craftsman, *trusting* his authority and superior experience. Indeed, the general public shares in the cultural transmission of such knowledge though acquiring a general understanding of the world, which includes evolution, relativity, quantum mechanics, and so on, without necessarily grasping the details of such concepts. Philosophers of science refer to this accepted scientific description of the world as a 'paradigm', which guides the scientist in distinguishing between facts and groundless assumptions. In contrast to the general public, the professional scientist appropriates this scientific tradition, learning to own it and validate it based on personal experience. So-called scientific facts, thus, are never simply 'given', but derive their significance from being integral parts of a certain holistic interpretation of the world.

Second, the scientist is not an independent observer, but inhabits the current paradigm and upholds it by her commitment. This commitment is by no means arbitrary, but derives from the pleasure of possessing a satisfactory understanding of the world we inhabit. Science thereby takes its place beside other explanations of our world, such as those found through art, religion, and literature. As in these humanistic disciplines, commitment to science derives from the basic satisfaction of knowing one's way around and achieving intellectual control over problems that arise. Another word for commitment is *faith*. Because an accepted paradigm is a reasonable, but never total, explanation of our world, scientists are personally invested and have faith in this world picture.

We have to dispel the illusion that scientists drop any theory about physics, astronomy, biology, or any other scientific subject that is not fully verifiable. The fact is that no paradigm manages to offer a total explanation of the world, and the scientist has to live with anomalies, that is, with experiences that do not fit the theory and threaten to undermine it. Their personal faith in the stability of a paradigm allows scientists to shelve anomalies in the hope of resolving them later through an expansion of the theory, and this indeed sometimes happens. At other times, however, persistent anomalies can lead to overthrowing an entire theory and opening a new way of understanding the world.

The physicist and historian of science Thomas Kuhn (1922–96) showed that the process of scientific discovery is not an orderly, rule-governed affair, but rather resembles a paradigm change Kuhn called 'scientific revolution'. Such revolutions occur when an older theory fails to explain new phenomena. To think of a scientist cheerfully trying this or that experiment, calmly changing course at each failure, distorts the dynamic and creative process of science, and occludes the scientist's deep commitment to a possible new theoretical framework. Often, this passionate commitment to an established paradigm will result in resistance to new theories. At other times, a researcher may be already committed to a new paradigm, but will not fully understand it until some additional discovery vindicates the new vision as a better account.

Scientific discovery depends heavily on the personal intuition of a scientist whose deep familiarity with a prior theory and the relevant facts, together with the hitherto stubbornly unexplained anomalies, allows him to *intuit* a better way of integrating all these particulars into a new coherent framework. This intuitive vision, while based on experience, cannot be reduced to logic, but constitutes an intellectual leap from one existing interpretive framework to another.

As the history of discovery from Copernicus to Einstein shows us, scientific discovery begins with intellectual visions by trained scientists, visions that were inspired by the beauty and elegance of a rational universe. We have said that the desire to understand and hence a basic curiosity are common to animals and humans. Yet we are also symbolic animals who are able to transmit, manipulate, and recombine information abstractly through signs, and thus capable of incomparable feats of the imagination. Science, too, relies on this capability, and indeed major discoveries depend on the use of deeply rooted pictures or metaphors about reality.

Let us not forget that one of the main inspirations of the astronomer Galileo, aside from his dislike of Aristotle's hold on the minds of theologians, was his belief that the Bible and nature were two books by the same author, God, and thus could not ultimately contradict each other. Thus, if science showed the earth to orbit the sun, there must be a better theological reading of the Genesis account than the traditional geocentric one championed by the current ecclesial establishment. What remains obscured by a still-popular myth in scientific circles is that Galileo's proof for a heliocentric universe did not undermine Christianity. In fact, many Christian scientists and interested theologians were thrilled to discover that the earth was not, as Aristotelian metaphysics had demanded, at the centre of the universe, where all matter had to go due to its base corporality, while noble and spiritual things soared upward. Galileo had shown to the contrary that our planet was liberated from this shameful position and joined the dance of the stars.

As we can see from this example, both in science and in theology, facts are important, but what ultimately matters is the theory or world picture by which we integrate the individual parts of what we know into a meaningful whole. Even experimental verification by itself is no guarantee for arriving at the correct interpretation of reality, as demonstrated by the well-known controversy on alcoholic fermentation.

In the 1830s, for example, a number of chemists found that fermentation was not a mere chemical reaction but due to the living function of yeast cells, that is, of living cellular organisms. These findings, however, went against the dominant intellectual vision of contemporary scientists, who had synthesized yeast from inorganic materials, and took such results as proof for their cherished project of a chemical approach to all living matter. Consequently, they mocked the other findings as a regressive lapse into a vitalism (the view that nature is an intelligent, living organism) they believed themselves to have overcome. For a long time, this controversy remained unresolved, and the great French chemist Louis Pasteur (1822–95), who sided with the organic camp, recognized that each side integrated the facts differently based on 'an order of ideas which, strictly speaking, cannot be irrefutably demonstrated'. Eventually, the discovery of intracellular enzymes showed that both sides had been correct: the catalyst of the fermenting reaction was indeed a chemical enzyme, which also proved to be a vital part of living yeast cells. In this case, two theories were transformed into a more comprehensive paradigm.

Science as a distinct mode of knowledge

The fermentation controversy demonstrates that scientific knowledge does not progress through gradual accumulation of verified experimental results nor through rigorous, impersonal observation and application of rules. Such mechanical operations remain an important part of scientific activity, but do not explain the actual nature of scientific knowledge or discovery. Instead, striving for coherence through the integration of particulars into a meaningful whole, science proceeds hermeneutically. Every supposedly neutral observation is theory-laden; that is, facts are selected and recognized according to a certain interpretive framework. A theory is like a lens through which the scientist sees something *as* something of value for science, just as the trained artist or historian recognizes techniques or compositions as valuable. In turn, every new scientific theory is a visionary act of the imagination that is inspired by observation of facts and grounded in received scientific practices. Scientific knowledge thus moves in a hermeneutic circle, moving between parts and whole, clarifying and often transforming one another.

We have seen that science depends as much on tradition, personal involvement, commitment, and intuitive insight as does any other mode of knowing. The creative and visionary side of science also aligns scientific activity with the creative arts, poetry, and literature. At the same time, however, science remains a distinct mode of knowing. As with every other knowledge discipline, natural science is an articulate explanatory system of human experience that is accepted and sustained by personal commitment.

Unlike religion or the arts, however, or unlike more abstract sciences such as pure mathematics, the natural sciences deal in their own particular way with the facts of experience. When a scientist envisions a new atomic model, we assume that something like atoms actually exist. When we read literary texts such as Tolkien's *The Lord of the Rings*, we don't expect to meet Hobbits in the British countryside. And yet the truth of fiction, too, corresponds to human experience. Fantasy literature tells us that life can be enchanted, and consists of more than mere matter in motion. These sentiments correspond to our experience, but the *validation* of literary truths by our experience is not exactly the same as the experimental *verification* required by science. Perhaps one way of putting this difference is that while both science and the arts proceed basically from faith (a tacit personal commitment to a world picture or interpretive framework) to understanding, the faith element in the arts is deeper, more emotionally intense and intellectually complex. Nevertheless, both scientific verification and aesthetic validation of experience testify to the same personal and interpretive quality of all human knowledge. To know is to interpret.

The future of hermeneutics

What is the future of hermeneutics? In our introduction we said that hermeneutics stands for interpretation in general but also for a philosophical discipline. In the general sense of interpretation, hermeneutics remains relevant as long as we seek to understand ourselves and our world. As a philosophical discipline, hermeneutics is a minor field in the academy, which is dominated by more analytic approaches to philosophy concerned with truth statements and their verification. Hermeneutics, by contrast, enquires into the conditions of understanding, and that is more important than ever, especially in light of our changing culture. Computing technology and virtually universal access to information are rapidly altering the way we perceive the world and we need to reflect on the impact of computing technology on the nature of understanding. Induction into language and culture was formerly a more communal enterprise, controlled by parents and teachers. Now, for the first time in human history, a whole generation is growing up in many parts of the globe for whom the world is predominantly mediated through computers, tablets, and smartphones. They are 'born digital', and one of the most important questions to address in the future will be how this technical revolution affects their interpretation of world and self.

Hermeneutics has a future insofar as it may help us assess the impact of digital technology on the conditions we have outlined in this book as essential for human understanding. We have learnt that understanding requires an engaged rather than a detached self. How we understand ourselves and the world depends on the practical relation we have to things and on the interpretive lens we acquire through our cultural upbringing. Does today's digital culture encourage detached or engaged selves? We have also seen that understanding requires the patience of sustained familiarity with a problem and an educated imagination through which we can imagine things differently. Does our digital culture increase or decrease our attention span? Does digital technology encourage the deep familiarity with one's tradition, whether secular or religious, necessary for intelligent dialogue with other traditions? Are digital natives habituated to the long-term indwelling of a topic essential to scientific innovations, social visions, and creative artistic works?

Finally, hermeneutic philosophy provides an important antidote to fundamentalism. Secular and religious fundamentalists still defend the modernist illusion of timeless, certain knowledge. Their shrill voices and defensive, sometimes even violent, stances toward others are driven by the fear of relativism. In contrast, by insisting on the interpretive nature of all human knowledge without falling into relativism, hermeneutics encourages the interpretive humility essential to any dialogue. Acknowledging the profound mediation of even our deepest beliefs through history, tradition, and language should induce us to admit that we could be wrong and are thus open to correction. The awareness that our own interpretive framework can benefit from another's encourages conversation in order to learn. By contrast, the belief that truth is something self-evident only an obstinate fool would reject fosters a basic stance of confrontation. Insofar as hermeneutic philosophy encourages conversation among those of different faiths and cultures, hermeneutics will remain an essential part of our future.

Appendix

This *Very Short Introduction* was written to demonstrate the essentially interpretive nature of human knowledge. To achieve this end, the volume focuses on showing the practical workings of hermeneutics in the main disciplines of knowledge. This focus on the practical did not allow us to deal with philosophical criticisms of hermeneutics, or to mention important hermeneutic developments. For the reader interested in these more abstract aspects of hermeneutics, this appendix sketches some of the most important debates concerning hermeneutic philosophy.

Safeguarding objectivity (Emilio Betti versus Gadamer)

The eminent Italian legal theorist Emilio Betti (1890–1968) was one of the first major critics of philosophical hermeneutics. Betti feared that Heidegger's elimination of the traditional subject–object division for interpretation opened the door to subjectivism. For Betti, texts are accurate representations of the author's mind (*mens auctoris*), whose originally intended meaning the reader should reconstruct through the use of reliable interpretive methods. Betti warned that Heidegger and Gadamer undermined such objective communication with their existential definition of the hermeneutic circle. For traditional philology, the hermeneutic circle pertained only to the inner workings of the text as an object to be analysed by a dispassionate, analytical reader. Chapters 2 and 3 of this volume describe how Heidegger and Gadamer extended this traditional hermeneutic circle of part and whole to include the reader's own subjectivity and cultural beliefs.

Betti argued that making the reader's own historical situation essential to interpretation would open the door to interpretive relativism, threatening especially the normative authority of legal and theological texts.

Betti saw this loss of objective meaning most clearly in Gadamer's claim that interpretation and personal application are inseparable. Betti insisted on a two-step approach to interpretation. First, the interpreter had to do the objective historical work of determining precisely what an author had intended to say and to judge how successfully the author had expressed his intention in a text. In a second step, the interpreter then applied the recovered meaning to her own context. Betti charged Gadamer with collapsing this distinction between the original meaning of an author's text and the significance of this meaning for the interpreter's present context. Gadamer replied that human consciousness does not divide interpretive activity into two steps of reconstruction and interpretation. Rather, application is always intrinsic to the interpretive process because even the historian must read a text from within his own cultural horizon and interests. Betti's criticism provided the basic platform for E. D. Hirsch's similar objections to Gadamer, which is described in Chapter 4.

Ideology criticism (Jürgen Habermas and Karl-Otto Apel versus Gadamer)

If we derive knowledge about ourselves and the world from our participation in our respective cultural traditions, what keeps us from merely repeating tradition uncritically? What mechanism allows us to achieve critical distance from these traditions and to detect ideological distortions of language and meaning? This was the question put to hermeneutics by the philosophers Jürgen Habermas (1929–) and Karl-Otto Apel (1922–). They agreed with Gadamer's critique of scientific objectivism, but they worried that he was too optimistic about tradition and the power of language to convey truthful insights about our human condition. After all, language and tradition can equally serve as instruments of manipulation and oppression. Thus Habermas and Apel contested the universal claim of hermeneutics that every aspect of knowledge is dependent on tradition. They argued that Gadamer emphasized too much the historical nature of human consciousness and paid insufficient attention to the need for critical reflection whereby we evaluate tradition in order to emancipate ourselves from dehumanizing social practices. They suggested that hermeneutics, as a description of how understanding comes about through our being in the world (i.e. an ontological description of understanding), requires a complementary critical evaluative dimension. Habermas and Apel thought that the social sciences could offer such a critical dimension. They modelled this critical function on psychoanalysis. A psychoanalyst takes an observing stance during communication with her patient in order to detect destructive beliefs stemming from deeply repressed traumatic experiences in the patient's past. In the same way, the social sciences provide a 'depth hermeneutic' for filtering out ideologically distorted communications (such as propaganda) and destructive cultural attitudes contained in traditions.

Gadamer replied that his hermeneutic philosophy was concerned solely with describing what happens when we understand. He dealt with the conditions for understanding and not with their moral evaluation. He merely wanted to show that all understanding depends on tradition and acknowledged authorities. If his description is correct, then Apel and Habermas were wrong to suggest psychoanalysis as a guardian of truth that is exempt from interpretation. For according to Gadamer, *every* evaluating judgement depends itself on some tradition and authority. Even in the suggested psychoanalytic scenario, the patient submits to the expertise of his doctor. Yet Apel's and Habermas's concern is certainly legitimate. How can we prevent blindness and even enslavement to bad traditions? Gadamer responded that the hermeneutic process itself contains a critical element. In his description of the hermeneutic circle, he insisted on the reader's task of shaping understanding according to the subject-matter presented by the text and thus of abandoning incorrect (*unsachgemäße*) pre-judgments in the course of interpretation. Interpretation thus becomes a constant process of revision and replacement in the quest for an ever more adequate understanding of a text. Moreover, tradition constantly changes because the reader always has to appropriate the past creatively. For Gadamer, critical reflection was thus an intrinsic part of the mediation between past and present that characterizes our historical existence.

Critical hermeneutics (Paul Ricoeur)

Along with Gadamer, Paul Ricoeur (1913–2005) was the most important hermeneutic philosopher of the 20th century. Ricoeur was already developing a hermeneutic view of knowledge in the contexts of Husserl's phenomenology, Heidegger's existential philosophy, Freudian psychology, and French language philosophy (called Structuralism) before he encountered Gadamer's book *Truth and Method*. Ricoeur's basic goal was to work out the proper relationship between the self and the objective semiotic structures (signs, symbols, texts) by which we communicate meaning and gain self-understanding. With Gadamer, Ricoeur upheld that all thought occurs in language, so that even our innermost reflections take place within linguistic structures we can analyse and interpret. Ricoeur thus mediated between Romantic and Structuralist views of interpretation. Against Romantic hermeneutics that advocated the reader's empathic identification with authorial consciousness, Ricoeur contended that the object of interpretation is not experience *as felt* by the author, but the *meaning* of such experiences as inscribed and traceable in linguistic and symbolic expressions. At the same time, he also rejected Structuralist theories that reduced the self to a passive channel of pre-existing language systems. For him, language does not speak—rather, people do. Similarly, Ricoeur wanted to combine critical views of language and the self as inherently unstable (advocated by the 'hermeneutics of suspicion' represented by Marx, Nietzsche, and Freud), with a basic trust in the reliability of meaning and its communication as found in ancient interpretation, but also in Husserl and Gadamer. Ricoeur argued that the masters of suspicion help us destroy naïve conceptions of unmediated contact with reality, thus asserting the need for interpretation. Yet this necessary critical detour is not the final state of affairs—lest one remain mired in scepticism—but forms merely part of the greater effort to grasp meaning more profoundly within a 'second naïveté'.

Ricoeur's criticism of hermeneutic philosophy was that Heidegger and Gadamer circumvent the necessary explanatory moment demanded by the linguistic structures we inhabit. They stressed intuitive understanding of a text at the cost of a verifying explanation of how we obtained our reading. Ricoeur agreed with Habermas and Apel that in their eagerness to criticize scientific objectivism, Gadamer focused too much on a pre-scientific, intuitive understanding conveyed through our immersion in tradition. This focus downplayed the important explanatory moment that allows us to validate our interpretations. Contrary to Apel and Habermas, however, Ricoeur did not advocate a regulatory science external to the hermeneutic process. Instead, he sought to combine understanding and explanation into one dialectical interpretive movement of *distanciation* and *engagement*. Distanciation requires linguistic analysis and a moment of critical reflection concerning the content of a text. In contrast to personal dialogue, the reader has to reconstruct an author's intended meaning using the linguistic-grammatical structures through which the author inscribed her views in a text that is no longer under authorial control. (Ricoeur calls this the text's 'semantic autonomy'.) This demonstrable process of explanation, however, is also one in which the reader *engages* the text's meaning based on his personal interest. What he engages, however, is not the consciousness of the author but the semantic world opened up by the text (see Chapter 4). In this way, argued Ricoeur, the appropriation of the text (what it means to me), occurs via analytical procedures that are neither mathematically certain nor relegate understanding to a merely arbitrary, subjective insight.

Hermeneutics, ethics, and deconstruction (Jacques Derrida)

Another major hermeneutic debate concerns the ethical dimension of interpretation. Most famously, the French philosopher, Jacques Derrida (1930–2004), described the hermeneutic impulse to understand another as a form of violence that seeks to overcome the other's particularity and unique difference. During a famous meeting with Gadamer in Paris (1981), Derrida suggested that behind the hermeneutic will to understand another lies an old metaphysical will to power, the desire to master and control difference. Hermeneutics' quest for meaning is thus really a quest for domination. While both Gadamer and Derrida derived their philosophies from Heidegger, Derrida claimed to have overcome the latter's residual 'logocentric' (i.e. reason or meaning-centred) thought patterns. Derrida's deconstructionist philosophy followed Heidegger in carefully tracing the history of philosophical concepts to question settled meanings. Derrida claimed, however, that Heidegger was still seduced by the desire for meaning when he searched for the significance of the question of Being. Derrida renounced such desire. Instead, he proclaimed himself a follower of the more radical hermeneutics of Friedrich Nietzsche (1844–1900), revelling in the play of endlessly deferred meaning. In ethical terms, borrowed from the French ethicist Emmanuel Levinas (1906–95), deconstruction is oriented toward radical hospitality that allows another to disrupt one's expectations and does not seek to interpret another's communication in order to assimilate his views to the framework of my own interpretive horizon.

Gadamer responded that his hermeneutic philosophy resisted the foreclosure of meaning just as much as Derrida's deconstruction, without, however, giving up the willingness to dialogue in an effort to understand one another. And, indeed, Gadamer's concept of interpretive horizon entails that one's own standpoint changes even as one understands another person or text more deeply. Certainly, the fusion of horizons that happens in understanding does integrate another's perspective into one's own, but not as a one-sided assimilation. When we understand another's viewpoint, even if we do not agree with it, our outlook has changed already. This essentially constantly progressing, open-ended hermeneutic process, however, requires ears open to another's voice. This willingness to listen, Gadamer countered, is necessary even for Derrida in everyday life, unless he wanted to live somewhere on an island in total isolation. But Gadamer did not just defend his hermeneutic, he also issued a challenge to Derrida. Gadamer turned the deconstructive tables by charging Derrida himself with crypto-Platonism: does not Derrida's own radical distrust of language and meaning evidence a hidden desire for an ethically pure state in which communication poses no risk? Is not his idea of irreducible otherness and difference beyond language and interpretation itself a Platonic desire for purity? In an interview towards the end of his life, Gadamer believed to have convinced Derrida that hermeneutic understanding is a transformative experience that does not assimilate another's meaning but allows for the constant revision of meaning. In 2003, Derrida himself, in a moving speech in Heidelberg, commemorating Gadamer's death, conceded that deconstruction as the disruption of sense and hermeneutics as the seeking of meaning are two equally needed sides in our human quest for truth. The Derrida–Gadamer debate has been continued into the 21st century by the Derrida acolyte John Caputo and the Ricoeur student Richard Kearney. While Caputo in his advocacy of 'radical hermeneutics' continued to defend unconditional hospitality and agnosticism about meaning, Kearney stood for 'critical hermeneutics'.

Kearney defended the need for hermeneutic discernment lest either guest or meaning to whom we open our door turn out to be monstrous and destructive.

Hermeneutics and pragmatism (Richard Rorty)

The American philosopher Richard Rorty (1931–2007) has been instrumental in making known Gadamer's philosophy in the English-speaking world. Gadamer's work helped Rorty sort out the problems he faced within his own tradition of analytic philosophy. Gadamer's emphasis on a historically shaped consciousness allowed Rorty to criticize the foundational belief in analytic philosophy that the human mind mirrors reality so that truth can be determined by rigorous linguistic analysis. In his seminal book, *Philosophy and the Mirror of Nature* (1979), Rorty thus interpreted Gadamer's axiom that 'being which can be understood is language', to mean that being is nothing but language. In the absence of any actual correspondence between thought and reality, truth for Rorty becomes simply what we interpret it to be. Formerly, philosophers thought of themselves as some kind of scientist whose concepts mirrored reality more or less adequately. Once we grasp, however, that our descriptions *construct* the meaning we give things, we realize that philosophers are not scientists but rhetoricians and poets who shape how we imagine life. Now, the tasks of philosophy and education are therefore no longer to come up with better descriptions of reality but rather to foster those interpretations of reality we deem the most edifying or useful for our society. As the Canadian hermeneutics scholar Jean Grondin pointed out, Rorty misappropriated hermeneutic philosophy for his own purposes. While it is true that Gadamer, following Heidegger, had opposed idealist notions of timeless innate ideas, Rorty's nihilistic inversion of this idealism is foreign to Gadamer's hermeneutics. For Gadamer, neither our language nor practice determines being. The whole point of his thinking is that being, an objective reality, discloses itself *through* language. Hermeneutics is thus closer to a critical realism than the kind of nominalist relativism Rorty advocated.

Hermeneutics and weak thought (Gianni Vattimo)

Another important hermeneutic development is the concept of 'weak thought' (*pensiero debole*) advanced by the Italian philosopher Gianni

Vattimo (1936–) in the early 1980s. Vattimo's view of hermeneutics is quite similar to that of Rorty, who, in fact, endorsed the term 'weak thought' in his own writings. 'Weak thought' denotes the claim that there are no 'strong' objective essential, timeless meanings. Hence interpretation does not represent pre-existent meaning but *generates* meaning. We don't discover the world through interpretation, but we create our world by describing and thus by interpreting it. For Vattimo, this interpretive quality of being is not relativism but our very chance at remaking our world in better ways. Weak thought thus becomes the very basis for human emancipation. For this reason, Vattimo also called weak thought 'good nihilism', because it breaks down or deconstructs the status quo. In his book, *After Christianity*, Vattimo linked his nihilistic hermeneutics to religion by explaining 'weak thought' in terms of God's self-emptying (*kenosis*) into history in the incarnation. On this view, secularization and the continual breaking down and weakening of supposedly timeless institutions such as religious or social hierarchies are all part of the incarnation's ongoing effect in history.

The influence of philosophical hermeneutics on theological interpretation

Theological debates about philosophical hermeneutics are essentially concerned with the mediation of divine revelation through human language and reason. Can human reason by itself obtain true knowledge of God and the most authentic life this God ordained for humanity? Judaism, Islam, and Christianity insist that finite human reason does indeed require divine revelation for understanding the purpose of life. Yet is revelation opposed to or compatible with reason? To what extent can reason, and that means philosophy, help interpret the divine message? In the 18th and 19th centuries, increasing confidence in reason apart from faith led to the gradual separation of theology and biblical exegesis. On the one hand, theology had become an intellectual exercise or the endless analysis of dogma, and theologians preached morality. Professional exegetes, on the other hand, were not guided by faith commitments but by a supposedly neutral, scientific method. They were essentially philologists and historicists, occupied with the historical and grammatical analysis of biblical texts in order to obtain the objective meaning of each textual unit. After two world wars, however, neither moral theology nor mere objective historical analysis—which advanced its own ideologically motivated interpretations under the cloak of neutral objectivity—satisfied peoples' need for religious and moral guidance. The Theologian Karl Barth (1886–1968) first gave voice to the need for God's revelation to speak once again in fresh ways on its own terms. Barth showed that the supposedly neutral historical–grammatical exegesis operated on an implicit rationalism that had created God in accordance with its own tame bourgeoisie vision of the Christian life. Barth's break with the theological moralism of cultural Protestantism required a renewed emphasis on revelation: God speaks to us through the Bible and the sermon in a way that shatters our comfortable cultural prejudices. Indeed, we need philosophy and critical tools for interpretation, but we cannot ever rely on them or allow them to limit how God may speak to us.

Barth thus emphasized *that* God speaks to the church but did not concern himself overmuch with *how* he does so. By contrast, the Protestant exegete, Rudolf Bultmann (1884–1976), who shared Barth's concern for divine revelation, focused on just this issue, and turned to philosophy for help. Bultmann drew heavily on Heidegger's work to analyse the existential conditions under which modern people could interpret and listen to God's revelation. Bultmann did not follow Heidegger's thinking uncritically, but he recognized in Heidegger's philosophy a call to authentic freedom that could connect modern readers with the gospel's invitation to authentic selfhood. Bultmann's whole programme of 'demythologization' was essentially an attempt to detect this biblical call to freedom in the mythical language of the New Testament.

Barth's and Bultmann's desire for a hermeneutics that allowed a modern person to listen anew to God's revelation in the Bible was continued in the next generation by the so-called 'New Hermeneutic' of Ernst Fuchs (1903–83) and Gerhard Ebeling (1912–2001). Bultmann had drawn on Heidegger's existential analysis of human life to depict theological hermeneutics as a quest for authentic existence in a modern world. Fuchs and Ebeling, by contrast, turned to the later Heidegger's focus on language as the most important medium for self-understanding. Heidegger had rejected analytic instrumental views of language for the view that language was the medium that disclosed our all important relation to Being and its call to us. This reference to Being in Heidegger is quite enigmatic, but his basic point is simple enough: what gives objects and human relations meaning is something that is greater than their sum total. Authentic existence requires that we do not make up reality but that we participate in something greater. This something greater shines through in our use and analysis of language.

Fuchs transferred this view to theology: Jesus's language of love in the New Testament is the true language of authentic existence under God. Thus interpreting the Bible is learning the authentic language of faith by trying to speak this language in life itself. Gerhard Ebeling differed from Fuchs in combining Heidegger's foundational view of language more strongly with Reformation theology. He focused on God's creative word of revelation as a 'word event' that speaks throughout history by constantly renewing itself. Theology, for Ebeling, is fundamentally hermeneutical because the very purpose of theology is critically to engage the text and our own presuppositions in order to allow God to speak. Thus, the New Hermeneutic combines philosophical and theological hermeneutics but also remains quite firmly subservient to the traditional Reformation doctrine of the Word: hermeneutics remains essentially a function of theology. Today, the importance of philosophical hermeneutics for theology and biblical studies is increasingly recognized among theologians of all confessions. In recent years, a number of biblical scholars have drawn on philosophical hermeneutics to advocate the renewal of explicitly theological interpretation.

References

Chapter 1: What is hermeneutics?

M. Heidegger, *On the Way to Language* (Harper & Row, 1982), p. 29.
Quotation from *The Apology of Socrates* 38a is from the Loeb Classic
Library edition.
C. Taylor, *Sources of the Self* (Harvard University Press, 1989), p. 21.
J. Macmurray, *Interpreting the Universe* (Humanities Press, 1996), p. 7.

Chapter 2: Hermeneutics: a brief history

M. Aurelius, *Meditations*, from the Everyman's Library (Knopf, 1992),
p. 45.
R. Descartes, 'Preface to the Reader', in *A Discourse on Method* from
the Everyman's Library, trans. John Veitch (Hackett, 1986), p. 6.
W. J. Goethe, *Faust*, trans. Albert Latham, vol. 1 (J. M. Dent & Sons,
1908), p. 31.
F. Schleiermacher, 'Monologen', in *Philosophische Schriften* (Union
Verlag, 1984), p. 72.
W. Dilthey, *The Formation of the Historical World in the Human
Sciences* (Princeton University Press, 2002), pp. 229 and 163.
M. Heidegger, *Ontology—The Hermeneutics of Facticity* (Indiana
University Press, 1999), pp. 4 and 14. This translation by John van
Buren does not capture the sense of 'Augen eingesetzt', the literal
putting in of eyes rather than merely opening them.
M. Heidegger, 'Poetically Man Dwells', in *Poetry, Language, Thought*
(Perennial Classics, 2001), pp. 211–27.

Chapter 3: Philosophical hermeneutics

H. Gadamer, *Truth and Method* (Bloomsbury Academic, 2013), p. 312. I have cited this edition as the only English version currently in print. The phrase 'the conversation that we are' is from this same edition, p. 386.

Plato, *Apology*, from the Loeb Classic Library (Harvard University press, 1962), pp. 68–145.

R. Pullins, 'Deathless Soul', in *Plato's Phaedo* (Focus Publishing, 1998), p. 97.

W. Shakespeare, *Othello* (Oxford University Press, 2006).

Chapter 4: Hermeneutics and the humanities

W. Shakespeare, *Hamlet* (Oxford University Press, 2008).

E. D. Hirsch, Jr, *Aims of Interpretation* (University of Chicago Press, 1976), p. 21.

E. D. Hirsch, Jr, *Validity in Interpretation* (Yale University Press, 1967), pp. 5, 47, and 106.

Chapter 5: Hermeneutics and theology

M. Ruthven, *Islam: A Very Short Introduction* (Oxford University Press, 2012), p. 21.

J. L. Esposito, *Islam: The Straight Path* (Oxford University Press, 2010), p. 19.

M. Ayoub, *Islam: Faith and History* (One World, 2004), p. 41.

The quotation 'an interpretation of its meaning' can be found in S. Murata and W. Chittick, *The Vision of Islam* (Paragon, 2006), p. xvi.

T. Ramadan, *Islam, the West and the Challenges of Modernity* (The Islamic Foundation, 2001), pp. 16–17.

Averroës, *The Book of the Decisive Treatise* (Brigham Young University Press, 2001), p. 19 (27.9–13).

F. M. Donner, 'The Historical Context', in *The Cambridge Companion to Islam* (Cambridge University Press, 2006), p. 23.

All scriptural references are from the New Revised Standard Version (Oxford University Press, 1998).

A. Neuwirth, 'Structural, Linguistic, and Literary Features', in *The Cambridge Companion to Islam* (Cambridge University Press, 2006), p. 97.

M. Ruthven, *Islam: A Very Short Introduction* (Oxford University Press, 2012), p. 40.

J. Brown, *Hadith* (One World, 2009), p. 3.

This 2007 reformist translation of the Quran is available from <http://www.studyquran.org/resources/Quran_Reformist_Translation.pdf>. The quote is from p. 11 of the pdf document.

T. Aquinas, *Commentary on Epistle to Galatians*, chapter 4, lecture 7, from the Aquinas Scripture Series (Magi Books, 1966), p. 138.

M. Luther, 'Assertio Omnium Articulorum Martini Lutheri Per Bullam Leonis X: Novissiman Damnatorum (1520)', in *Lateinisch-Deutsche Studienausgabe: Der Mensch vor Gott*, vol. 1 (Evangelische Verlagsanstalt, 2006), p. 81.

M. Luther, 'Prefaces to the Old Testament', in *Luther's Works*, vol. 35 *Word and Sacrament* (Fortress Press, 1960), p. 236.

R. Bultmann, 'New Testament and Mythology', in *Kerygma and Myth: A Theological Debate* (Harper & Row, 1961), pp. 3 and 32.

J. Green, *Practicing Theological Interpretation* (Baker Academic, 2011), p. 4.

Chapter 6: Hermeneutics and law

S. Pufendorf, Preface to *On the Duty of Man and Citizen* (Cambridge University Press, 1991), pp. 6–13.

R. Dworkin, *Law's Empire* (Belknap Press, 1986), p. 7.

J. Austin, *Lecture on Jurisprudence*, in *The Philosophy of Positive Law* (John Murray, 1885), p. 214.

J. Austin, *The Province of Jurisprudence Determined* (John Murray, 1832), p. 209.

H. L. A. Hart, *The Concept of Law* (Oxford University Press, 2012), pp. 107, 98, and 139.

D. Patterson, *Law and Truth* (Oxford University Press, 1999), p. 68.

H. L. A. Hart, *The Concept of Law* (Oxford University Press, 2012), p. 109.

A. Scalia, 'Common-Law Courts in a Civil-Law System: The Role of United States Federal Courts in Interpreting the Constitution and Laws', in *A Matter of Interpretation* (Princeton University Press, 1998), p. 13.

Chapter 7: Hermeneutics and science

F. Bacon, 'Novum Organum', in *The Philosophical Works of Francis Bacon* (Routledge, 2011), p. 261.

P. Laplace, *A Philosophical Essay on Probabilities* (Wiley & Sons, 1902), p. 4.

N. R. Hanson, *Patterns of Discovery* (Cambridge University Press, 1958), p. 19.

T. S. Kuhn, *The Structure of Scientific Revolutions* (University of Chicago Press, 2012), pp. 92–110.

D. Danielson, *The Book of the Cosmos: Imagining the Universe from Heraclitus to Hawking* (Perseus, 2002), p. 150.

Further reading

Chapter 1: What is hermeneutics?

W. Jaeger, *Paideia: The Ideals of Greek Culture*, 3 volumes (Oxford University Press, 1943–5).

B. A. Kimball, *The Liberal Arts Tradition* (University Press of America, 2010).

J. Macmurray, *Interpreting the Universe* (Humanities Press, 1996). Written completely jargon free, this set of philosophy lectures explains the interpretive nature of human knowledge.

Chapter 2: Hermeneutics: a brief history

L. K. Dupré, *The Enlightenment and the Intellectual Foundations of Modern Culture* (Yale University Press, 2004).

R. E. Palmer, *Hermeneutics: Interpretation Theory in Schleiermacher, Dilthey, Heidegger, and Gadamer* (Northwestern University Press, 1969).

Chapter 3: Philosophical hermeneutics

H. G. Gadamer, *Philosophical Hermeneutics* (University of California Press, 2008). While not a substitute for reading *Truth and Method*, this brief essay collection provides essential elements of Gadamer's hermeneutic philosophy.

J. Grondin, *Introduction to Philosophical Hermeneutics* (Yale University Press, 1994). The best scholarly introduction to this topic.

R. Palmer, *Gadamer in Conversation* (Yale University Press, 2001). Contains an interview of Gadamer by Carsten Dutt, which provides easy access to Gadamer's hermeneutic philosophy.

L. K. Schmidt, *Understanding Hermeneutics* (Acumen, 2006). A reader-friendly, jargon-free introduction to the basic figures and ideas of philosophical hermeneutics.

Chapter 4: Hermeneutics and the humanities

N. Frye, *The Educated Imagination* (Indiana University Press, 1967). These radio lectures are still among the best defences of literary studies and their essential role for society.

J. P. Ricoeur, *Hermeneutics and the Human Sciences: Essays on Language, Action, and Interpretation* (Cambridge University Press, 1981).

M. Terras, J. Nyhan, and E. Vanhoutte (eds.), *Defining Digital Humanities: A Reader* (Ashgate Publishing, 2013). A great essay collection on trends in the digital humanities.

J. Weinsheimer, *Philosophical Hermeneutics and Literary Theory* (Yale University Press, 1991). An essential text for understanding the relation of hermeneutics to literary studies.

Chapter 5: Hermeneutics and theology

J. A. C. Brown, *Hadith: Muhammad's Legacy in the Medieval and Modern World* (Oneworld Publications, 2009).

J. L. Esposito, *Islam: The Straight Path*, 4th edition (Oxford University Press, 2011).

Angelika Neuwirth. *Scripture, Poetry, and the Making of a Community. Reading the Quran as a Literary Text*. Oxford: Oxford UP, 2014. For the last decades, Neuwirth has spearheaded an international effort by Islam scholars to read the Quran historically and thus contrary to the established tradition.

M. J. Gorman, *Scripture: An Ecumenical Introduction to the Bible and its Interpretation* (Hendrickson Publishers, 2005).

J. B. Green, *Practicing Theological Interpretation* (Baker Academic, 2011). For those interested in the nuts and bolts of theological interpretation and its critique of historical criticism, this is the clearest explanation on the market.

W. Jeanrond, *Theological Hermeneutics: Development and Significance* (SCM Press, 2002). At roughly 200 pages, the best

introduction to the history and main issues in theological
hermeneutics.

J. L. Kugel and R. A. Greer, *Early Biblical Interpretation* (The
Westminster Press, 1986).

A. C. Thiselton, *Hermeneutics: An Introduction* (Eerdmans, 2009).
The foremost theological voice on hermeneutics and theology
offers a detailed survey of past and current views on this topic.

M. Westphal, *Whose Community? Which Interpretation?* (Baker
Academic, 2009). Written for the non-specialist, this book outlines
the importance of philosophical hermeneutics for theology.

Chapter 6: Hermeneutics and law

J. Arthur and W. H. Shaw, *Reading in the Philosophy of Law* (Pearson,
2009). Provides current essays on all aspects of and different
positions on legal theories and problems.

G. Leyh, *Legal Hermeneutics: History, Theory, and Practice*
(University of California Press, 1992). An older collection of essays,
but still a great introduction to the interpretive nature of legal
practice.

D. Lloyd, *The Idea of Law* (Penguin, 1991). This work provides
historical and comparative overview of all major concepts and
issues relating to the meaning of law.

Chapter 7: Hermeneutics and science

M. Polanyi and H. Prosch, *Meaning* (University of Chicago Press,
1996). Building on Polanyi's Gifford Lectures, *Personal Knowledge*,
this book extends the hermeneutic nature of science to the
humanities.

E. G. Slingerland, *What Science Offers the Humanities: Integrating
Body and Culture* (Cambridge University Press, 2008). Not an easy
read, but a rare attempt to show how body and mind interact to
interpret reality.

Index

Index

Index

SOCIAL MEDIA
Very Short Introduction

Join our community
www.oup.com/vsi

- Join us online at the official Very Short Introductions **Facebook** page.
- Access the thoughts and musings of our authors with our online **blog**.
- Sign up for our monthly **e-newsletter** to receive information on all new titles publishing that month.
- Browse the full range of Very Short Introductions online.
- Read **extracts** from the Introductions for free.
- Visit our library of **Reading Guides**. These guides, written by our expert authors will help you to question again, why you think what you think.
- If you are a teacher or lecturer you can order inspection copies quickly and simply via our website.